D1617091

AUTOBIOGRAPHIES IN EXPERIMENTAL PSYCHOLOGY

Edited by
Ronald Gandelman
Rutgers University

Frank A. Beach
Fred S. Keller
Howard H. Kendler
Karl H. Pribram
Curt P. Richter

LEA LAWRENCE ERLBAUM ASSOCIATES, PUBLISHERS
1985   Hillsdale, New Jersey   London

Lawrence Erlbaum Associates, Inc., Publishers
365 Broadway
Hillsdale, New Jersey 07642

Library of Congress Cataloging in Publication Data

Main entry under title:

Autobiographies in experimental psychology.

   Proceedings of a symposium held by the Rutgers
University Dept. of Psychology in the spring of 1983.
   1. Psychology, Experimental--Congresses. 2. Psychology, Physiological--Congresses. 3. Experimental
psychologists--United States--Biography--Congresses.
I. Gandelman, Ronald. II. Beach, Frank Ambrose,
1911-   . III. Rutgers University. Dept. of
Psychology. [DNLM: 1. Psychology, Experimental--
congresses. 2. Psychology, Experimental--personal
narratives. BF 181 A939 1983]
BF181.A87 1985   152'.092'2   85-20585
ISBN 0-89859-544-4

Printed in the United States of America
10 9 8 7 6 5 4 3 2 1

Contents

Preface

Individuals generally are invited to participate in symposia in order to remind the audience (and readers should the proceedings be published) of their past accomplishments and to apprise them of their current research endeavors. The addresses, then, involve the presentation of data, old and new, and their placement within a theoretical framework. We have sponsored a number of such events concerned with various specialty areas within psychology.

When time drew near to organize our latest symposium it was decided to alter its goal and, thus, its format. Instead of bringing together individuals for the purpose of sharing data-related information, we decided to ask our participants to share their lives and thoughts about the future of the discipline; to share insights which come only from looking upon long, productive, and innovative careers. What we had in mind is best expressed by the following excerpt from the letter of invitation:

> The Rutgers University Department of Psychology is initiating a symposium series commencing in the Spring of 1983. Each focusing upon a particular research area, the symposia will consist of addresses by investigations who have made significant and enduring contributions to the study of behavior. The initial symposium will focus upon animal and human research in the area of physiological-experimental psychology. You are asked to address two general issues. One, autobiographical in nature, concerns the factors which led to your interest in the study of behavior, and in particular, to the research directions you followed. The second issue concerns the future of psychology, that is, your thoughts concerning fruitful avenues of present and future research; in other words, what you think research psychologists will be doing—or ought to be doing—a decade from now.

We were delighted when Professors Frank Beach, Fred Keller, Howard Kendler, Karl Pribram, and Curt Richter accepted our invitation.

Their remarks are presented in this volume for which I found myself serving as editor. While pleased to have my name associated, even if only on a book cover, with those of the participants, I must confess that I edited nothing. The reason for that inactivity should be obvious. My function was simply that of forwarding agent, compiling the manuscripts and sending them to the publisher. It should be mentioned that due to illness Professor Richter unfortunately was unable to attend the symposium. His remarks, therefore, are presented here for the first time.

A successful symposium requires the expenditure of a great deal of energy and money. The former was provided by a number of individuals including graduate students, staff and faculty. Special thanks are given to Mrs. Jean Natarelli and Herbert Hauser. Funds were generously provided by Dr. Kenneth Wolfson, Dean of the Graduate School. We also wish to thank Dr. Edward J. Bloustein, President of the University, and Dr. Ruth Ellen Bloustein, for their gracious hospitality.

Ronald Gandelman
Rutgers University
New Brunswick, N.J.

Introduction to
Frank A. Beach

A number of people asked me if they could introduce Frank Beach. As organizer of the symposium I exercised my perogative and answered "no" to each of them in order to save the honor for myself. It is a rare opportunity to be able to introduce someone who not only is a productive and innovative scientist but who also was instrumental in establishing a field of research. I refer, of course, to behavioral endocrinology.

Frank Ambrose Beach was born in Emporia, Kansas on the 13th of April, 1911. He received the B.S. and M.S. degrees from Kansas State Teachers' College after which he spent a year teaching high school English. Following two years as a research assistant in neuropsychology to Karl Lashley, he entered the University of Chicago from where he obtained the Ph.D.

Dr. Beach's employment history includes Curator and Chairman of the Department of Animal Behavior, American Museum of Natural History, Professor of Psychology, Yale University and the University of California at Berkeley. He is now Professor Emeritus at the latter institution. He has received numerous awards such as an honorary D.SC. from McGill University, Distinguished Scientific Contribution Award from the American Psychological Association, and the Fifth Carl G. Hartman Award for Research in Reproductive Physiology, to name a few. Dr. Beach also is a member of the National Academy of Sciences.

If I had to characterize Frank Beach's research in a few words, I would call it "consistently significant." By this I mean that his research was (and is) designed to illuminate important issues, leaving subsequent parametric analyses to others. The publication in 1948 of his book *Hormones and Behavior* was the first major synthesis of data and theory concerning the involvement of the endocrine system in behavior. He has since published many theoretical papers which have markedly influenced the course of research. Also, he founded and edited the journal *Hormones and Behavior*.

I could continue to describe Frank Beach's contributions to behavioral endocrinology and to psychology in general. But at this point I think we would rather hear from him.

Ronald Gandelman

Howard Kendler (L) and Frank Beach

1 Conceptual Issues In Behavioral Endocrinology

Frank A. Beach
University of California, Berkeley

If the talk I have prepared for this occasion seems to reflect a strong schizophrenic tendency you must not hold me acountable. The cause lies in the nature of my assignment. I quote from the letter inviting me to participate in the present symposium.

> Each participant is asked to address two general issues in his talk. One, autobiographical in nature, concerns the factors which led to your interest in the study of behavior, and in particular, to the research directions you have followed. The second issue concerns the future of psychology, that is, your thoughts concerning fruitful avenues of present and future research; in other words what you think research psychologists will be doing—or ought to be doing—a decade from now.

I will deal briefly with my professional history, partly because I do not understand it very well, but mostly because I would rather spend my allotted time discussing the future rather than the past.

LOOKING BACKWARDS

My professional development resulted from a sequence of conscious and unconscious choices leading to progressive narrowing of focus and increasing specialization. Perhaps "choice" is too definite a term. It is closer to the truth to say that I more or less "waffled" my way from one situation to another, and then another, and then to

5

another until finally I found myself working entirely in the field of behavioral endocrinology.

The first step was developing an interest in psychology. As an undergraduate I thought study of this subject would help me to understand human beings, particularly myself. Of course it did nothing of the sort; but by the time I discovered that error my interest had narrowed to experimental psychology, which I viewed then as the ultimate in science. Laboratory experiments on the learning and forgetting of nonsense syllables might not expand my understanding of human nature in general; but I could at least solve some practical problems facing every college student.

Eventually I decided that human learning was so complex that I would never understand it; but white rats were simpler, and perhaps I could still solve the basic problems if I shifted to animal learning. The psychology department at the Kansas State Teacher's College where I was enrolled had never had an animal lab; but I received permission to start one. Once I became involved with animal behavior I developed a new interest in physiological psychology.

I was particularly excited by research then being published by Karl S. Lashley at the University of Chicago. He was studying learning and memory in rats before and after he removed parts of their cerebral cortex. "At last," I thought, "here is the way to the truth! Now we can discover how the brain really works. Now we can finally solve the mind-body problem!"

So I went to Chicago, studied under Lashley, and became a dyed-in-the-wool neuropsychologist. But before I could start my Ph.D. research, Lashley moved to Harvard, and I was left without a mentor. Nevertheless, I wanted to do an experiment on brain function. I definitely did *not* want to work on learning. It seemed as if every budding physiological psychologist was jumping on that bandwagon.

Instead I chose to study what was then popularly referred to as "innate" or "unlearned" behavior. The word "instinct" had recently become taboo. For the thesis I investigated effects of cortical lesions on maternal behavior in rats. It turned out that the neocortex is not just for learning; but also is involved in the organization of instinctive behavior (Beach, 1937).

Lashley thought enough of my thesis to offer me a research position at Harvard at the modest salary of $75 per month. In the depth of the depression very few teaching positions were open, so off I went to Cambridge, where I proceeded to do some experiments on effects of brain lesions on mating behavior of male rats. About midway through the project I happened to describe the results to another chap in the lab near mine who was a graduate student in endocrinology.

I told him that when I removed large amounts of the cerebral cortex from male rats they stopped copulating with receptive females. He asked if the brain-operated males had normal testes. I had no idea. I was interested in the front end of the beasts, not in their posterior organs. The endocrinologist pointed to the possibility that extensive brain injury might result in disturbance of pituitary secretion which in turn could lead to functional castration.

I hadn't the faintest understanding of what he was talking about; but after reading a bit of endocrinology I decided to inject some of my brain-operated, de-sexed males with testosterone just to see what would happen. Parenthetically, I might as well confess that is about as close as I ever came to using strong inference in the design of an experiment. Nevertheless, lo and behold! The injected rats regained their libido; and I thought I was on the way to a Nobel Prize.

Loss of brain tissue destroyed the sex drive, and injection of male hormone restored it. I waited in vain for that call from Stockholm; but in any event I had taken the final step. I didn't know it at the time but my career for the rest of my life had been settled.

In the succeeding five or ten years I did fewer and fewer experiments on brain function, and more and more on hormones and behavior. Without planning, without external direction and with no professional background for the speciality, I had become a Behavioral Endocrinologist; and since then I have never been anything else.

FUTURE DEVELOPMENTS IN BEHAVIORAL ENDOCRINOLOGY

Now comes the time to look into the crystal ball. Since my primary allegiance is to behavioral endocrinology and not to psychology as a whole, my interest in the future centers on the former. It is easy to predict numerous advances in technology and in the expansion of empirical evidence; but rather than indulging in prophecy I prefer to discuss a few problems that I believe behavioral endocrinology must solve if it is to raise its status from that of a research specialty and become a full-fledged scientific discipline.

It is my conviction that the necessary changes will not be achieved by borrowing techniques from cellular biology, neuroendocrinology, endocrinology proper, or any other more advanced field, even though this practice has greatly benefitted behavioral endocrinology in the past. Neither is it likely to result from continued prosecution of atheoretical, data-oriented research on hormones and behavior.

Establishment of facts is a primary responsibility of any scientific discipline; but facts alone do not make a science. They are only the warp of science. The woof consists of general principles, unifying concepts and testable theories. In the absence of these, the continuing accumulation of empirical evidence produces a chaotic overload of information; of itself useless and uninterpretable. It is my fear that behavioral endocrinology is moving rapidly in this direction.

If this fear is justified; if such a regrettable condition does exist, we have brought it upon ourselves. To compensate for the current imbalance, behavioral endocrinologists must begin to pay more attention to broader intellectual and theoretical issues.

New concepts are needed that will achieve several essential objectives. One pressing need is the development of a coherent intellectual schema or framework in terms of which evidence already available can be classified, organized, and integrated. Fullfillment of this need would provide a foundation for achievement of a second objective, namely the identification of basic versus trivial problems, and development of a sense of orientation that could provide guidance for future research.

Concepts of Behavioral Endocrinology as a Discipline

It might be helpful to begin thinking about behavioral endocrinology in terms of its eventual disciplinary status. Defining fields of science is a risky enterprise, particularly if the definition is overly exclusive. Nevertheless, there is potential value in working definitions that are recognized as temporary, flexible, and open to repeated modification. In this sense I suggest the following definition as a starting point.

> Behavioral endocrinology is a biobehavioral science which deals with relations between the endocrine system and organismic behavior, placing special emphasis upon their functional or adaptive significance, their mediating mechanisms, and their ontogenetic and phylogenetic history.

The number and nature of modifications others may want to make in this definition are immaterial. My point is that in our daily research, as well as in efforts to formulate unifying concepts or theories, it is useful to arrive at some concensus regarding the scope and objectives of behavioral endocrinology, and to visualize its relations to other biological sciences.

Alfred North Whitehead once asserted that the last thing to be discovered about any discipline is what that discipline is all about. Philosophers sometimes express their thoughts in hyperbole, but in this statement there is more than a grain of truth. Perhaps it is true because scientists become so immersed in day-to-day details of their research that they take little time to ponder its most general implications. Certainly I detect very little evidence that individuals conducting research on hormones and behavior are overly concerned with what behavioral endocrinology is all about.

My conviction is that behavioral endocrinology represents an attempt to discover ways in which the endocrine system helps all kinds of animals, including our own species, to "make a living," to survive, and to perpetuate their kind. I take it as axiomatic that the most profound questions that can be asked about behavior are how it contributes to the universal functions of individual survival and species reproduction.

If this view is accepted, then the first-order questions in behavioral endocrinology are those dealing with behavior most immediately relevant to these functions.

Concepts of Behavior

Very broad definitions such as the one I have proposed for behavioral endocrinology are of little value unless there is general agreement on the meaning of the component terms. In the present instance it is crucial to arrive at a clear understanding as to what is meant by "behavior."

Stimulus-Response Definition.   Webster's International Dictionary defines behavior as follows: "anything that involves action and response to stimulation." This is the S→R model that has been favored in behavioral endocrinology since research began. It is an effective and powerful model that has led to many important discoveries about hormones and behavior.

Without the S→R model very little progress could have been made in establishing some of the most basic facts in behavioral endocrinology. It will continue to serve an essential function in all future research. And yet there are important theoretical and practical problems to which it is not applicable; and for this reason we need a supplementary or companion model that conceptualizes behavior in a different perspective.

Interactional or Transactional Definition.   When we observe behavior as it occurs under natural circumstances we do not observe reactions of individuals to various stimuli. Instead we observe *interactions* between the organism and various features of its environment.

I can illustrate the point by reference to a familiar type of experiment. Suppose I decide to study the importance of testosterone in mating behavior of the male ring dove. I record the male's behavior before castration, after castration, and again after my castrated subject has been treated with testosterone. But what is it that I actually observe? It is a temporal pattern of interactions between my experimental male and a female ring dove. I am not actually viewing effects of hormonal manipulations on the male; but rather their effects upon a sequence of reciprocal social interactions or activities which I have defined as "mating behavior."

Alteration in the male's hormonal status affects his stimulus properties as far as the female is concerned; and these changes in turn alter her reactions to him. When the female's reactions are modified she becomes a different kind of stimulus to the male, and so on ad infinitum.

Practically all examples of organismic behavior involve actions of the organism that alter its environment. For example, testosterone causes the male frog to utter his mating call (Kelly & Pfaff, 1976). His vocalization attracts a gravid female; and thus the male's social environment is modified. Estrogen induces the female canary to engage nest building (Hinde & Steel, 1975). As construction of the nest proceeds, the bird introduces into her own environment a new source of stimulation.

To diagram actions of organisms upon their environments we can use the symbol O→E.

It also is obvious that the environment exerts effects upon the organism. In birds such as the arctic penguin, hormones necessary to initiation of nest building are not secreted unless material suitable for nest construction is present in the environment (Roberts, 1940). A special vocalization by male swine, known as the "chant de coeur," induces the estrous sow to adopt the mating posture (Signoret, 1967). Male dogs are stimulated to urinate by the odor of urine from other males (Dunbar, 1978). The male dove's courtship cooing evokes ovarian development and behavioral changes in the female (Cheng, 1979). When the female canary builds a nest, the resulting structure becomes a new stimulus that eventually elicits oviposition by the female.

Actions of the environment upon the organism may be represented by the symbol E→O.

In the most comprehensive sense, behavior embraces both of the symbols I have described, and it therefore is appropriately diagrammed as O↔E. In other words, behavior includes both actions of the organism on the environment and actions of the environment on the organism. The O↔E model represents an interactional or transactional definition of behavior. It can also be classified as an ecological definition.

Such definitions are not new to psychology. In fact they have been proposed as alternatives to the S→R model. John Dewey emphatically denied that behavior can be dichotomized into stimuli and responses (Dewey, 1896). Kurt Lewin's influential theories of personality and social behavior were based on the concept that individuals react to a surrounding field in which potential sources of stimulation have different valences determined by internal characteristics of the individual (Lewin, 1935). J. R. Kantor's physiological psychology dealt with "interbehavior" of organisms and stimulus objects in a specific field (Kantor, 1947). B. F. Skinner originally defined behavior as, "that part of the functioning of an organism which is engaged in acting upon or having commerce with the outside world" (Skinner, 1938).

Acceptance of the interactional or transactional model of behavior could have far-reaching effects on the development of behavioral endocrinology. It would suggest, for example, that *the most basic questions in the field do not deal narrowly with effects of hormones on organisms, but with ways in which hormones influence interactions between organisms and their environments.*

Concepts of the Environment

But what do we mean by the term "environment." Is it simply everything, every object, every source of energy in the space that environs, or surrounds, the organism? Surely not, because organisms vary from one another in sensory capacities. The eyeless cavefish has no visual environment; and that of the little brown bat resounds with ultrasonic echoes that are absent in our own environment.

Furthermore, even when sensory capacities are comparable, given features of the so-called environment have different behavioral significance for different organisms. Cabbage butterflies and leopard frogs possess efficient visual systems, but their visual environments are different, partly because the ocular systems are different, but more significantly because the two species *perceive* or interpret the same physical stimuli in quite different ways.

For example, the pattern and coloration of a flower have no behavioral significance for the frog; but they control the butterfly's feeding and oviposition behavior. A crawling fly is behaviorally irrelevant and therefore ignored by the butterfly; but it is immediately captured as food by the sticky tongue of the frog.

More than 40 years ago, a German zoologist, Jacob von Uexküll pointed out that even when they exist side by side, a man and a wood louse inhabit two entirely different worlds. Instead of "worlds," of course, von Uexküll used the German term "Welten"; and he proposed that the word *Umwelt* be given the special meaning of "self-world." To quote his definition, the Umwelt comprises, "the perceptual and effector worlds together that form the closed unit within which each animal lives" (Uexküll, 1930).

Inclusion of the "effector world" is important. It implies that an organism's environment is partly defined in terms of responses the individual is capable of making to different aspects of its surroundings.

Another salient aspect of von Uexküll's definition of Umwelt is that it includes the "perceptual world" instead of just sensory stimuli from the environment. Except in the case of simple reflexive reactions, organisms respond to the perceived environment, and this involves preliminary processing of sensory information. The distinction is important to behavioral endocrinology, because one of the most common ways that hormones affect behavior is by modulating the individual's perception of environmental variables.

Concepts of Mediating Mechanisms

My final conceptual issue pertains to identification of mechanisms that mediate correlations between hormones and behavior. The first experimental studies of such correlations were conducted during the second half of the nineteenth century by physiologists who, quite naturally, postulated physiological mediators. For example, different workers argued that secretions of the testes influence mating behavior of male fowl (Berthold, 1849), and rats (Steinach, 1910), by modifying functions of the nervous system.

The first psychologists to become involved in such research often employed psychological constructs as explanatory devices. Thus, the decrement in mating behavior that follows castration in male rats was interpreted as a consequence of lowered sex drive (Stone, 1939).

As behavioral endocrinology grew, and particularly as technological progress was made in neuroendocrinology, neurophysiology, and cellular biology, the search for mediating mechanisms centered more and more upon specific areas in the brain. I have argued previously that the general concept of such mechanisms should be broadened to include extraneural, peripheral organs and structures essential to effective conduct of behavioral responses (Beach, 1971).

Whether the focus is central or peripheral, study of physiological mechanisms involved in relating hormonal and behavioral variables is an important scientific enterprise; and one that has provided a great deal of very important information.

I believe, however, that development of theory in behavioral endocrinology could be greatly enriched if the concept of mediating mechanisms were explicitly expanded to include psychological processes or variables as well as those of a physiological nature. In fact it would be well if the two categories were given equal status.

To clarify the issue, as I see it, let me offer specific definitions. Physiological variables are physical entities or processes, actually or potentially open to direct observation. Typical examples are structures such as cells, tissues, and organs; and processes such as conduction of nerve impulses or secretion of glandular products.

Psychological variables have no physical existence. They are theoretical constructs. The only properties they possess are those of the empirical data from which they are derived. They are defined operationally. Familiar examples are sensation, perception, emotion, learning, memory, and attention.

A very important characteristic of psychological variables is that they stand on their own two feet, so to speak. Their validity does not have to be established by reducing them to a physiological level. They are validated in terms of behavior, which represents a higher level of organization than that represented by separate physiological variables.

It is, of course, a legitimate and important scientific procedure to investigate the *physiological correlates* of psychological variables. For example, a great deal of valuable research has been aimed at identifying putative changes in the brain associated with the processes of learning and forgetting. But the constructs of learning and memory have their own independent validity, and are open to analysis on a purely behavioral level with no physiological referents whatsoever.

To repeat for the purpose of emphasis, what I am suggesting is that constructs such as learning, memory, perception, and the like be formally recognized as possible mediating mechanisms in behavior endocrinology. It may be objected that considerable research is presently devoted to study of hormones and learning (McGaugh, 1983). The observation is correct but irrelevant.

The research to which it refers is aimed at discovering how hormones influence learning and memory, but not how learning or memory may be involved in modulating relations between hormones and behavior.

In a typical learning experiment the effects of a hormone on acquisition and retention of a new response are studied by administering the hormone before, during, or after acquisition of the response. The next step may be an attempt to identify loci in the brain at which the hormone acts to exert its influence.

If we wish to use the construct of memory as a variable intervening between a hormone and performance of some behavioral response, a different approach is involved. It has been demonstrated by numerous experiments that young male birds of some species learn local variants or dialects of the species song while they are fledglings, when they themselves are too young to sing, but are constantly exposed to the songs of adult males. If a young male is reared in auditory isolation after exposure to adult song, he will, when he reaches maturity several months later, begin to sing. Initiation of song coincides with and depends upon secretion of testosterone. After a few days of practice, but still in auditory isolation, the male reproduces the full species song, dialect and all (Marler, 1970).

Relations between rising testosterone levels and utterance of song are mediated by many mechanisms including growth of the syrinx and its associated muscles, as well as by changes in special brain nuclei associated with song production. However, in the absence of experience gained during early exposure to adult males' singing, the local dialect does not appear. For this reason it seems not only justifiable but necessary to include memory of that experience as one important variable mediating the correlation between testosterone and the eventual song pattern.

My talk will be completed after I describe one example in which perceptual processes can be treated as a mediating mechanism; but first I must define perception, which I will do by quoting Howard Bartley.

> Whereas sensation is defined in relation to sensory mechanisms, perception is regarded in terms of the tasks imposed on the organism by the nature of the environment. Each of the perceptual systems is composed of the cooperative action of several sense mechanisms and extracts information from the environment (Bartley, 1972).

An important aspect of this definition is its ecological implications. It emphasizes relations between the perceiving organism and its environment, and thus is consonant with the O↔E model of organismic behavior.

There is a large body of evidence suggesting that hormones can affect social perception in human beings. It is based on studies of women during different stages of their menstrual cycles. Emotional changes at particular times in the cycle have been examined in many circumstances by many investigators. Cyclic changes may seem absent in some individuals, but in others they are quite predictable and obvious to the woman herself as well as to her associates.

According to Judith Bardwick (1976), many women experience changes in emotional tone just before menstruation when estrogen levels are low, and also after menstruation when progesterone levels are high. However, Bardwick believes that instead of recognizing the psychological changes within themselves, some women assume it is the outside world that has changed.

For example, if an acquaintance makes a personal remark intended to be humorous, it may be taken as a slight or an insult by the woman in her premenstrual period, but recognized as a pleasantry in the postmenstrual or luteal phase of her cycle. In other words, the same social stimulus is perceived in one way under certain hormonal conditions, and in the opposite way when other hormones prevail. The woman's behavioral reactions will vary according to the way in which she interprets the social stimulus. Thus can perceptual processes be considered as mediating mechanisms which are influenced by hormones and, according to this influence lead to different kinds of behavior.

Now I find that I have come full circle. I began by describing my early interests in psychology. Then I explained the events leading to my conversion to behavioral endocrinology. And finally I discover myself arguing in favor of psychological constructs as variables intervening between hormones and behavior. The evidence plainly indicates a severe case of confused identity. But the malady doesn't worry me for a moment. No matter what I am, or how I got here, it has been a lot of fun getting here, and the road ahead looks challenging and exciting.

REFERENCES

Bardwick, J. M. Psychological correlates of the menstrual cycle and oral contraceptive medication. In *Hormones, Behavior and Psychopathology*, E. J. Sacher, Ed., N.Y., Raven Press, 1976.

Bartley, S. H. *Perception in Everyday Life*. N.Y., Harper & Row, 1972.

Beach, F. A. The neural basis of innate behavior. I. Effects of cortical lesions upon the maternal behavior pattern in the rat. J. Comp. Psychol., 24:393–436, 1937.

Beach, F. A. Hormonal factors controlling the differentiation, development and display of copulatory behavior in the ramstergig and related species. In *Biopsychology of Development*, L. Aronson & E. Tobach, Eds., N.Y., Academic Press, 1971.

Berthold, A. A. Transplantation der Hoden. Arch. Anat. Physiol., 16:42–46, 1849.

Cheng, M. Progress and prospects in ring dove research: A personal view. In *Advances in the Study of Behavior*, J. S. Rosenblatt, R. A. Hinde, C. Beer, Eds. 9: 97–129, N.Y., Academic Press, 1979.

Dewey, J. The reflex arc concept in psychology. Psych. Rev., 3:357–370, 1896.

Dunbar, E. F. Olfactory preferences in dogs: The response of male and female beagles to conspecific urine. Biol. Behav., 3:273–286, 1978.

Hinde, R. A. & E. Steel. The dual role of daylength in controlling canary reproduction. Symp. Zool. Soc. Lond., 35:265–278, 1975.

Kantor, J. R. *Problems of Physiological Psychology*. Bloomington, Principia Press. 1947.

Kelley, D. B. & D. W. Pfaff. Hormone effects on male sex behavior in adult South African clawed frogs. Horm. Behav., *7*:159–182, 1976.

Lewin, K. *A Dynamic Theory of Personality.* N.Y., Harper, 1935.

Marler, P. A comparative approach to vocal learning: Song development in the white-crowned sparrow. J. Comp. Physiol. Psychol. Monog., *71* (2):1–25, 1970.

McGaugh, J. L. Hormonal influences on memory. Ann. Rev. Psychol., *34*:297–323, 1983.

Roberts, B. The breeding behavior of penguins. *Brit. Graham Land Exped. 1934-1937, Sci. Reports:*195–254, 1940.

Skinner, B. F. *The Behavior of Organisms.* N.Y., Appleton-Century, 1938.

Steinach, E. Geschlectstrieb und ect sekundoxre Geschlectsmerkmale als Folge der innersekretorischen der Keimdrusen. Zentralblat. f. Physiologie, *24*:551–570, 1910.

Stone, C. P. Sex drive. In *Sex and Internal Secretions,* E. Allen, Ed., Williams & Wilkins, Baltimore, 1939.

Signoret, J. P. Attraction de la femelle en oestrus par la male chez les porcins. Rev. Comp. Anim., *4*:10–12, 1967.

Uexküll, J. von. *Die Lebenslehre.* Postdam-Zurich, 1930.

Introduction to Fred S. Keller

Introducing Dr. Fred S. Keller is sufficient to make the day of any hard-core behaviorist. It is doubly sweet to do it on an occasion when we are asking him to give us his reflections and projections on the science of psychology just 10 years after the publication of the second edition of his book, *The Definition of Psychology.*

Fred Simmons Keller was born in 1899. He obtained his B.S. degree in 1926 from Tufts College (University), his M.A. in 1928 from Harvard University and his Ph.D. in 1931 as well from Harvard. He then taught at Colgate University until 1938 and at Columbia University until 1964. He was a Fulbright-Hays Professor at the University of Sao Paulo in 1961 and Professor of Psychology at the University of Brasilia in 1964. He then taught at Arizona State University for three years and at Western Michigan University for five years. In 1973, he held the Cecil H. and Ida Green Honors Chair at Texas Christian University and from 1974 to 1977 was a Distinguished Visiting Psychologist at the Center for Personalized Instruction of Georgetown University. Since 1980 he has been Adjunct Research Professor of Psychology at the University of North Carolina in Chapel Hill.

Dr. Keller is the author of several books on psychology, stretching from *Principles of Psychology* (with W. N. Schoenfeld) in 1950 to *Pedagogue's Progress* published in 1982. His many articles encompass diverse concerns: from delayed response in the chimpanzee in

1934 to the current "Getting-old behavior." While perhaps best known and much appreciated by the current crop of young professionals for his original work in personalized instruction, one should recall his pioneering research on oxygen deprivation and conditioning in the white rat, light-aversion in the same organism, and the selective reinforcement of spaced responses (known later and widely utilized as the DRL schedule).

In 1917, he left school to become a Western Union telegrapher and this experience resulted in his extensive research on radio-operator training in World War II for which he received a *Certificate of Merit* from President Truman in 1948. Among others honors, he served as President of the Eastern Psychological Association in 1957, received the Distinguished Teaching Award from the American Psychological Foundation in 1970 and won the Distinguished Contributions for Applications of Psychology Award from the American Psychological Association in 1976. He holds honorary degrees from Long Island University (C. W. Post), the Institute for Behavioral Research, Colgate University, and Western Michigan University.

Whether he is addressing the intricacies of the control of animal behavior, code acquisition, or the development of the personalized system of instruction known as the Keller Plan, the power and simple grace of his style of experimentation and exposition form a behavior system of gentle elegance and enlightened application. It is best typified by a quote from near the end of his *The Definition of Psychology:* "The unity in multiplicity which system can achieve may even be described as beauty." I give you Fred Keller.

John L. Falk

Fred S. Keller

2 Experiments I Have Known

Fred S. Keller

My first reaction when invited to take part in this symposium was one of pleasure. How nice to be a member of such a distinguished group; what an opportunity to consider my research and place it in historical perspective! As for guessing about the future, which I was also asked to do, surely I would think of something.

Then I had some second thoughts. Looking at my list of publications, I discovered 10 experimental studies, only four of which I carried out alone. If I added extra-laboratory studies, almost all of them collaborations and in the area of training, the number would be more than doubled, but this wasn't basic research.

So I regretfully decided to decline the invitation. I wrote a letter to that effect, but I didn't send it. Perhaps I should have, but I got to thinking about the studies that I hadn't published, the studies done by others in which I played a minor part, and the studies that came out of group endeavors that I helped to set in motion. If I reported some of these, together with my own, maybe I could justify my presence on the panel. It would be, at any rate, an autobiographical attempt, which had been suggested. So I wrote and got permission, and here I am today.

Several factors led me to the study of behavior. As an undergraduate at Tufts College, I attended classes in logic, ethics, and philosophy with a behavioristic teacher—Robert Chenault Givler, a pupil of

23

E. B. Holt and a friend of E. R. Guthrie—who had considerable effect upon my thinking. The first book that I read in psychology, in 1925, after leaving college, was John B. Watson's *Psychology from the Standpoint of a Behaviorist,* a book that I bought to help me as a printing salesman. This led me back to college for another year and on to graduate school at Harvard, financed by a part-time teaching job at Tufts.

One of the courses that I taught, from 1926 to 1929, was in Comparative Psychology, and the textbook that I used was Watson's *Behavior*—an excellent introduction to that field. I drew my lectures mainly from Washburn's *Animal Mind,* which covered the phylogenetic realm in detail, extracting the mental reference as I went along.

An eminent behaviorist came to Harvard as a visitor in 1928, in the person of Walter S. Hunter, then a professor at Clark University in Worcester, Massachusetts. I attended his course of lectures and his seminar in animal behavior. He made behaviorism come alive for me and determined for nearly a decade the main direction of my teaching and research.

Professor Hunter was well known for his introduction of two research procedures, each related to the concept of "symbolic process" or "representative function." In 1913 he studied the *delayed reaction* in rats, dogs, raccoons, and children. In each case, the subjects were rewarded when they went correctly to that one of several places at which a light had earlier been presented. In this experiment, rats and dogs were able to choose correctly only when they had "pointed" toward the proper one of three locations throughout the period of delay. Children and raccoons, however, had successfully responded after short delays even when they were disoriented within the waiting period. To explain the findings from these subjects, Hunter argued for "an unknown intraorganic cue nonobservable to the experimenter"—a "representative factor" like that of "sensory thought," which enabled the subjects to respond correctly when the guiding stimulus was no longer present.

Four years later, Hunter studied the delayed reaction of his daughter, a 17-month-old child, in a two-choice situation, and found her able to bridge delays of 20 seconds or more, although distracted during the period of delay. The representative factor was now described as probably kinesthetic, the equivalent of gesture language, having its locus in the bodily musculature and appearing phylogenetically and ontogenetically in advance of vocal language.

(Watson had said of the delayed reaction that vocal language was essential.)

By 1928, Hunter had attacked another problem and developed another method. Beginning with the possible intrusion of "position habits" in animal discrimination studies, he was led to ask about the rat's ability to learn a series of right or left responses at the choice point independently of external stimulation, such as that of light or sound. For example, could an animal master a simple left-right-left-right form of alternation on successive runs in a discrimination apparatus when there were no outside cues to guide him?

The answer to this question was a *yes*. As early as 1920, it was clear that rats could easily master a simple alternation. But when Hunter tried to teach them a so-called *double* alternation, in which they had to choose in a left-left-right-right-left-left fashion, the animals were unsuccessful after many, many trials. No better results were gotten when the discrimination apparatus was made into a "temporal maze," permitting the animals to make successive choices without the need for handling after every run, and when the number of daily choices was reduced to four—left-left-right-right or right-right-left-left. Other variations in procedure were also without effect. Hunter finally concluded that it was impossible for white rats to solve the problem, just as they had failed to make correct delayed responses.

While at Tufts in Medford, Massachusetts, just a bicycle ride from Cambridge, I got successful short delayed responses from two children in a two-choice situation, confirming Hunter in his earlier study and going somewhat lower in the age scale, well before a vocal language had developed. I never tried to publish this experiment, but I got an A on my report to Hunter.

A third experiment provided data for my doctoral dissertation. Four white rats were given daily training throughout a ten-month period on an elevated temporal maze, 25 feet long, two feet wide, and 19 inches from the floor. Two of the animals had the double-alternation problem of making left-left-right-right choices. For the first four months they were rewarded only when four choices had been made (the daily trial). For the remainder of the time, food was given for each run of the series. The reason for making the maze so long was to permit a greater accumulation of sensory effects throughout the runs; and the reason for rewarding every run was to make the practice situation similar to the one that Hunter used with his raccoons.

Two other rats were given training on the right-right-left-left problem for the first part of the study. Then they were transferred to other problems in order to determine the presence of factors that might hinder progress with the double alternation. One such factor was an apparent tendency of the animals to respond with a simple left-right alternation in their choices.

My first two rats were able to solve the double-alternation problem. Although unstable in performance, they each outdid the three raccoons in Hunter's study. I blamed the instability upon the lack of sensory input from successive runs, as well as the counter tendency to simple alternation, and I concluded that the problem was one of sensory discrimination. Measurements of choice-point "indecision times" for the successful subjects, as well as data from the others, were considered to support the view that the symbolic-process explanation was unnecessary.

My doctoral dissertation was never offered to a journal. Perhaps it's just as well; some of my discussion seems confusing to me now. At any rate, I had been working almost daily from August until June and was exhausted. I never wanted to handle another rat. The college year was over; I was getting ready for a move to Colgate University and my first full-time position; and I had no thought for other matters.

At Colgate, where I stayed from 1931 to 1938, I had $25.00 yearly for research and a large room on the top floor of Alumni Hall for laboratory space. As soon as I became adjusted to the scene, I bred a little colony of rats, enlisted half a dozen student helpers, and started my career. Several minor studies were completed in the next few years and my research interests underwent a basic change.

The first experiment that I undertook at Colgate was with the help of Clarence W. Young, another new member of our Department, who built the apparatus for me. I studied double alternation in another temporal maze, one in which white rats went *up* or *down*, rather than right or left, at the point of choice. The results obtained were even better than monkeys had provided in a 1930 study by Louis Gellermann in Hunter's laboratory. I felt confirmed in my belief that a simple right-left bias was an obstructive factor in the earlier double-alternation studies with the rat.

In another study, I repeated an experiment by Harry Harlow on the social facilitation of eating in the rat, but got different results. When I wrote to Harry with the news, I expected him to point out errors in my replication, but he answered only that he hadn't thought much of his study anyhow. I was flabbergasted, but I did not attempt to publish my results.

James C. Welch, a Colgate senior, made a study of delayed reaction in a German Shepherd dog, and was able to demonstrate a good performance in a two-choice situation, without the need of a persisting bodily attitude throughout the period of delay. This contrasted with the early findings, but when we tried to publish the results, we were told that one subject was not enough.

With Lyndon M. Hill, another senior, I repeated a maze experiment by E. C. Tolman and C. H. Honzik on "insight" in white rats. We reached a non-"insight" conclusion, arguing that the animals in their experiment had simply failed to make a visual discrimination, and offering supportive data from our study. This research was published, but I don't believe Professor Tolman ever read it. At least he never mentioned it to me.

In 1935, I bought a 45-dollar box from Ralph Gerbrands, then the Harvard shop-man in the Psychology Department. It was delivered to me, complete with a lever-and-food-dispenser unit, on April 29th, 1932, in Cambridge. It had been designed by B. F. Skinner, a friend and former Harvard classmate. According to my diary, I left Cambridge on May 1st, with the box and ten Wistar rats, at 4:15 P.M., arriving at Hamilton, N.Y., exactly 8 hours later. A colleague in the Physics Department at Colgate made a cumulative recorder for me and I had a new research device.

The first experiment that I did, with several student aides, was to study the rate of lever pressing when a rat got all its meals within the box, receiving a single pellet of food whenever a response was made. This study was inspired in part by Curt P. Richter's observations of activity and eating, but what impressed me most in our experiment was the kind of eating records that we got. The animals ate at irregular intervals during the day and night, as we expected, but gave us straightline curves on each occasion, unlike the ones obtained when they are fed but once a day and the eating rate declines throughout the session. I have never fully explained this difference.

In another experiment, aided by another student, I studied the rate of lever pressing in three groups of rats while on different schedules of deprivation. A 22-hour daily deprivation produced the best rate results and maintained body weight throughout the 10-day period of investigation. An important feature of this study, as well as others with our Skinner Box, was the ease with which we got "good" results under "bad" conditions. There was neither light, nor sound, nor temperature control; the box was always open at the top to permit refilling of the pellet-vending apparatus; and my assistants, although willing, were untrained—even more than I was. Yet our records of behavior were as regular and reliable as those obtained in highly controlled experiments with the best of technical assistance.

I took my Skinner Box with me to Columbia University in 1938, when I was given another instructorship and better facilities for research, or so I hoped. Also in that year, Skinner sent me a copy of a treatise that he had written, *The Behavior of Organisms,* a book that was to guide my teaching and research from that time on.

The instructorship was satisfactory, but the facilities for research were slow in coming. Professor Warden, who sponsored all the animal experiments, had no room for me on the second floor of Schermerhorn Extension. The first study that I carried out was in my home, with my 17-month-old daughter as a subject; the second was on Schermerhorn's third floor, in a Barach Portable Oxygen Chamber, in an experiment with Clifford P. Seitz on oxygen deprivation and conditioning in the rat.

My daughter behaved as I had expected, like the rat, and I saw no need to publish the results, though I reported on them at a local meeting; the low-oxygen study also came out well, with clear effects upon our rats, but further research was abandoned when Dr. Seitz, the expert in low-oxygen matters, took a job at Alabama. I was, however, given laboratory space in Professor Warden's bailiwick and began to think of new experiments for my Skinner Box.

The Columbia story has two parts. One concerns my own research, which was very small in quantity and was interrupted during World War II. The other deals with studies that I helped to generate throughout a period of nearly 20 years, but which I cannot claim as mine. In the time I have today, I'd like to mention two of my experiments and their relationship to the larger scene.

The first of these may have stemmed unconsciously from several other observations. One was the comment of a blind student, Michael Supa, when we entered my Colgate Laboratory room one evening and I turned on the light. He told me that my rats were quieter when the light was on. Another was Curt Richter's finding on the nocturnality of rats; and still another was Burrhus Skinner's observation that response rate was depressed by light. For reasons such as these I may have asked: Is light removal reinforcing for albino rats?

Four white rats were given daily sessions in my Skinner Box. The top of the box was covered only with a plate of glass and a shallow baking dish that has been filled with water. Whenever an animal responded when a student lamp was lit above the glass, I turned the light off for 60 seconds, after which I turned it on again until the next response. And so on. Each animal was soon conditioned to turn off the light. Later on in the experiment, I used an intermittent schedule of reinforcement and studied the effect of different intensities of light. I got orderly results from each of my experimental subjects. This study was perhaps the first to deal with the rate of an escape response.

I reported on this light-aversion at a meeting of psychologists on December 6th, 1941, in Massachusetts, the day before the Japanese attacked Pearl Harbor. I had little time for rat research throughout the next four years, which I devoted mainly to problems of Morse code learning, at Columbia and at a Signal Corps training center in Missouri. I did have time, however, to get perspective on my teaching, in its relation to my systematic bias and to Skinner Box research. This led me finally to propose a different sort of first-course offering at Columbia—a laboratory course that took account of reinforcement theory and the ease with which behavior principles could be demonstrated under very crude conditions.

The plan was readily accepted, equipment was prepared, and a laboratory was set up, mainly by John Volkmann, my partner in the undertaking. The course with launched in the fall of 1946, with the aid of William N. Schoenfeld, when Volkmann left Columbia for Mount Holyoke. Within another year, the undergraduate curriculum was revised to follow up the first course, two more laboratories were set up, and more assistants were employed, as well as a new instructor.

From the viewpoint of our students and our staff, as well as the administration, our offering was successful, and a number of our colleagues, like Professors Hull and Yerkes, applauded our endeavors. However, we were not without our critics, in the University and elsewhere. We were described as cultists in our narrowness of viewpoint and our zeal; we were said to have deprived Columbia sophomores of their birthright; and I think that someone mentioned the Pied Piper, piping the children to disaster. (There were no *white* rats in Hamelin Town.)

Whatever the validity of these assertions, they are irrelevant in the present context. Our curriculum generated research and researchers.

Laboratory exercises led to undergraduate projects; projects sometimes led to Masters' essays, to doctoral dissertations, and to experimental programs. There was an atmosphere of exploration and
discovery everywhere, with everyone involved—students, assistants, and instructors. Our assistants' meetings were a source of pilot
studies, new proposals, and revisions in our thinking. There were
shared ideas and cooperative ventures.

In a first-year laboratory experiment on light-dark discrimination
in our rats, with reward for lever pressing in the light and no reward in
darkness, it was noted that our animals continued to respond in
darkness now and then, even after several hours of training. Someone
suggested that such responding might be accidentally rewarded
sometimes because it happened just before the light came on. One of
our assistants carried out a study in which the positive stimulus, the
light, never came on immediately after a response in darkness. The
procedure was effective in getting rid of lever pressings in the dark.

This observation led to an exploration, in another laboratory
course, of the effect upon response rate of simply introducing a 15-
second period of non-reward in every minute, with all the other lever
pressing reinforced. This led, in turn, to a systematic study by M. P.
Wilson and myself of spaced responding (known today as *drl*—
differential reinforcement of low-rate responses).

Three white rats were our experimental subjects, each with its own
Skinner box, a window which permitted us to watch the animals'
behavior during the experimental sessions. We reinforced our animals with food for all responses that followed other responses after a
certain number of seconds—10, 15, 20, 25, and 30, in different
phases of the study. The rats developed very good time discriminations and the rate of their responding decreased in a linear fashion as
the intervals were lengthened.

An error in placing the subjects in their boxes led to the observation that each of them had developed a series of responses other than
lever pressing throughout the periods of delay. Rat No. 1 went to the
water bottle after reinforcement, poked its nose through the food-cup
opening, and went back to the water bottle before returning to the
lever; No. 2 turned away from the bar and groomed, poked its nose
through the food-cup opening, and then went back to the lever; No. 3
climbed on the water bottle and then to the ventilation holes in the
rear of the cage, after which it poked the glass cover of the cage and
returned to the lever. These actions varied with the interval of delay,
but were stereotyped enough to identify each rat.

Shortly after our experiment, we learned about an elaborate investigation of inter-response times by a former pupil, Douglas Anger, at Harvard University, using pigeons. I believe that Anger's dissertation became a point of departure for many later studies of the differential reinforcement of low-rate responding.

An informal follow-up of our Columbia study was carried out by Douglas Ramsey, my assistant. He used a nine-year-old boy as his subject, pressing a telegraph key as a response, a 10-second interval of delay, and a penny for each response that turned on a signal light behind the key. The boy developed an excellent time discrimination, as well as a theory of how he earned each penny. "It's magic," he said, "After you get a penny, you start at the edge of the table, creep up very slowly, and hit the key: It works most every time."

A dining-room extension of this method was conducted with my 13-year-old son, a tape recorder, a tin cup, and a supply of pennies. He was asked to utter words (not sentences) as he looked about the room. I selected one of these and dropped a penny in the cup 10 seconds after each time it was uttered. He made a very good time discrimination, of which he was unaware, and he filled each interval with a loosely connected series of words that he thought I wanted him to learn.

My 17-year-old daughter, in similar circumstances, filled the intervals with words relating to a coming high-school examination, but did not establish any clear-cut chains. Columbia College students, tested by George Geis, a graduate assistant, tended to disclose their major fields of study in their choice of words.

Another spaced-responding study was carried out by Lawrence Stoddard, a Columbia Teachers College product, with children and a lever-pressing apparatus, within a playroom situation in Washington, D.C. His subjects filled the intervals by counting pictures on the wall, singing, dancing, sitting on their hands (that was Murray Sidman's little boy), and other forms of waiting.

I always have regretted that no clinician ever undertook to use the drl procedure in therapeutic practice. If Carl Jung could use reaction times in a word-association test as part of his procedure, why couldn't someone make a test of "time discrimination" (preferably in the darkness) to disclose the themes of most importance in a patient's verbal repertory!

Our final treatment of drl was made by Eli E. Kapostins, in his doctoral research, using Wagner College students, five different intervals of delay (7 to 47 seconds), and a small amount of money as reinforcement. Some of the informal observations were confirmed, but others weren't. Different kinds of "waiting behavior" were observed, in addition to a certain degree of verbal chaining. When Kapostins changed the word to be rewarded on a given schedule, the subjects made a quick adjustment, indicating that the reinforcement strengthened more than just the "right" response. Unlike our findings with the rat, the *rate* of making all of the responses remained quite constant in spite of alterations in the length of the inter-response time.

The early work on light aversion led to further experimentation at Columbia in the forties and the fifties. Techniques of stimulation and recording were improved by Volkmann, H. M. Parsons, and Michael Kaplan. Systematic studies were carried out by Kaplan on light intensity and response rate, and the method was extended by Ralph H. Hefferline to the study of avoidance behavior in the rat. Murray Sidman, one of our early Ph.D.s, took a revision of the procedure to the Walter Reed Army Medical Center in order to study shock avoidance, after light-aversion proved to be too weak a source of motivation for his needs.

I have cited two examples of research in which I played a part at Columbia in the forties, fifties, and the sixties. There were others that I could have added, but the majority of experiments in those years were ones in which Nat' Schoenfeld took an active part. After him, Ralph F. Hefferline was an important member of the team, along with William W. Cumming, who was added to our staff in 1958. Both men died while still productive workers, Cumming in 1969 and Hefferline in 1974.

The experiments to which we lent support within the fifties were in several different fields. The unconditioned rate of lever-pressing (we named it "operant level") was first explored by Hefferline in his doctoral investigation of avoidance and followed up by Schoenfeld with the aid of two collaborators, Joseph Notterman (now at Princeton) and Philip Bersh (now at Temple). Studies of repeated conditioning and extinction were begun by Donald H. Bullock (later at Catholic University) and followed up by Joseph A. Antonitis (now at Maine) and George B. Kish (who took his doctorate at Duke and is now, I think, at Roanoke College).

From the acquisition and elimination of behavior, interest at Columbia turned within the fifties to the *maintenance* of behavior. Different reinforcement schedules were explored by M. P. Wilson

(Bell Laboratories), John J. Boren (American University), Jack D. Findley (?), Michael Kaplan (U.S. Army, in London), J. Gilmour Sherman (Georgetown University), Thom Verhave (Queens College), and several others whose names escape me now.

An analysis of *operant discrimination* was the subject matter of F. C. Frick's doctoral research in 1948. (Frick, now retired, became Director of the Lincoln Laboratory at M.I.T.) His work was followed up by James A. Dinsmoor (Indiana University), who related the discrimination problem to conditioned reinforcement and to motivation. *Conditioned (secondary) reinforcement* was the theme of further studies by Schoenfeld and collaborators, as well as C. B. Ferster's doctoral research.

A flurry of experiments in the forties and the fifties dealt with *chaining*. Some of these were inspired by studies elsewhere, some by studies of our own, and still others by a combination of the two. Runway experiments at Yale had led to a distinction between homogeneous and heterogeneous chaining—the linkage of similar or of dissimilar S-R units. Skinner had said, in 1938, that "when a reinforcement depends upon the completion of a number of similar acts, the whole group tends to acquire the status of a single response." Schlosberg and Katz had demonstrated successful up-down and right-left double alternation of the lever-pressing response with rats, explaining it as the fusion of a sequence of responses into a single pattern—a fusion made more readily, they asserted, because the responses came so close together.

At Columbia, in our study of spaced responding, we were led to the notion of "superstitious" chains of response with which our subjects filled their intervals of delay. This notion found support, as I have noted, in later studies using human subjects. Also, an exploration by Charles Ferster showed that rats, when asked to press a lever twice for each reward, tended to be successful when the two responses were unlike. When they appeared to be the same, they were generally followed by at least one more response before the animal approached the food tray. When reinforcement was discontinued, the animals went on with doubles for much of the experimental session.

These observations were followed up by Justin Carey in a doctoral study wherein the interval between the two responses was reduced to a quarter of a second. Two groups of animals were given lengthy training in doubles and in singles, but in different order, after which they were given 15 daily periods of extinction. Animals trained with doubles last, reverted finally to singles; those trained last with singles responded first with singles, then with doubles, and finally again with singles. Carey related his findings to the psychoanalytic concept of regression.

A related group of experiments, by Robert Berryman, Frances Mechner, and William Wagman, were concerned with the rat's capacity to respond to its own responses, or to their sensory consequences. Two levers were employed. Following a given number of responses on the right-hand lever, for example, a single response on the left-hand lever would be reinforced. Minimal runs of 4, 8, 12, and 16 responses on the right-hand lever were employed.

Orderly distributions of run length were provided by each rat; they varied with the minimal requirement; their accuracy improved with training; and was greater for the shorter runs. My only regret concerning these experiments is that I didn't ask for a double-alternation sequence—two responses on the right-hand lever, followed by two responses on the other. It would have rounded out a circle that began in 1931 at Harvard in my doctoral research. As it is, however, I must be content with an approximation and bring this section of my story to its end.

In the studies I have listed here, the names attached were those of young researchers who did the major portion of the work described and, according to standard practice, received the major credit. It should be recognized, however, that in a group like ours, composed of many persons—teachers and assistants, even students—engaged in almost daily interaction, it was often difficult to state the source of any project with assurance. More often than not, I think, multiple causation was the rule. It also seems to me that there were more ideas for research than anyone had time to carry out. This is probably the sort of thing that happens when a field of study has just been opened up for exploitation with a new technique.

Footnote: The names that I have mentioned in this section of my talk have been exclusively those of men. This need not imply a policy of sexual discrimination. Maressa Hecht (Orzack), Dorothy Hubbard (Gample), Leila Kern (Cohen), Carol Eckerman, and Maria Amelia Matos did their work with us, but in other spheres than I have treated here. Helen Kaplan, Julia Hall, and Beatrice Lane came across the street from Teachers College to carry out their animal research with us. Ruth Morris (Bolman) and Evelyn West were successively my assistants, but left the University before their graduate work was done. Anne Ritter was my "reader" in our introductory course. And so on. There were others, too, whose names I don't remember now.

Most of our young researchers in the forties, fifties, and the sixties at Columbia went into academic life. Some of them are now at the peak of their careers; others have retired or are about to do so; and a few have died. Many changes have occurred since they began their studies: There are new developments in research equipment, including the ubiquitous computer; there are new experimental subjects (the pigeon has replaced the rat as the animal of choice); there are new departures in experimental method (*auto-shaping*, for example); there are new concepts, new problems, and new "laws." The horse-and-buggy days are gone. No longer does one sit beside a Skinner Box with a pellet in his hand, watching a white rat depress a lever, while a pen or pencil makes a cumulative record on the paper of a slowly turning drum. No longer does one look at the behavior of his subjects.

I haven't tried to keep up with these changes since 1964, and I probably could not have done so anyhow. I was slipping behind before the date of my retirement. Many of the studies now reported in our journals are beyond my comprehension. So I am hardly qualified to talk about the present scene in behavior science, let alone discuss its future. Yet, in my invitation to take part in this symposium, I was asked not only to look backward, but to look ahead, to express myself on "fruitful avenues of present and future research . . . what you think research psychologists will be doing—or ought to be doing—a decade from now."

At the time I received the invitation, I thought it would be easy to look into my tea leaves and come up with something. Surely there were things that I could say about the future, and who could prove me wrong, at least within my lifetime? But when I reached this stage of my discussion, I found myself in trouble. I had forgotten that the "future" was a decade, which is hardly any time at all for a person as mature as I am. I shall do the best I can, however.

1.   Within the next ten years, I expect that we shall find continued use of the computer in the management of experiments and the treatment of their data. I hope this doesn't mean, however, that the problems we attack will be determined by this tool or by the fact that

we have access to it; and I hope the metaphors that it provides will not delude us into thinking that they tell us something new about behavior.

2.   Within the decade I predict that someone will announce the existence of a law, mathematically formulated, to which someone else will take exception. This will be the source of several papers.

3.   Within this time frame, too, several behavior analysts will uncover cases of "cognition" which readily fit within a behavioristic formulation. Several congitivists will uncover cases that do not, and at least one textbook writer will assert that the disclosures aren't in conflict.

4.   Experimentalists in this period will continue to draw away from nonexperimentalists in the A.P.A., and from behavior modifiers in the A.B.A. The A.B.A. will continue to draw away from the A.P.A.

When I look into the distant future—to the year 2050, for example—the greatest change I see within our science is an unprecedented growth of interest and investigation within the field of language—verbal behavior, that is—at every stage of human life from childhood to old age, in all its forms and manifestations. Through extension of the simplest principles of behavior, we have already made considerable progress in the fields of mental retardation, rehabilitation, psychotherapy, community life, and education. Verbal behavior itself has already been interpreted in the light of reinforcement theory, with provocative results. By 2050, I believe, interpretation will have given way to experimentation, with results that have a bearing on many fields of learning. It seems to me that I can even now perceive some little steps in that direction.

This field has been neglected, I believe, for insufficient reasons: the fear, perhaps, of having to cope with specialists in neighboring disciplines—philosophers, philologists, logicians, lexicographers, and linguists, for example. "For fools rush in," said Pope, "where angels fear to tread." No one wants to be a fool. Others may feel the threat of being stigmatized as subjectivists, cognitivists, dualists, or worse, by participation in such studies; and all of us have had a history of single-organism research, whereas verbal behavior, almost by definition, is a social matter.

The enterprise will be advanced, I think, by great improvement in the educational process, which already has begun. By 2050, I am sure, group instruction in our schools will have been replaced throughout the entire range of education, in every major discipline, from its beginning to its end. The effect upon the quality of our final product at the highest levels is certain to be great.

The behavior scientists of tomorrow will be better trained, and sooner, than the behavior scientists of today. They will have come up through the system on different tracks, perhaps, but with success at every stage of progress and will have passed through their apprenticeship with leaders in their fields. They will not be called upon to give instruction in the customary sense of classroom lectures. They may work alone or as members of whatever groups that they may choose. Their work will be maintained by institutions in which research facilities of the highest order are of easy access. Continuance of access will depend upon the use they make of the facilities and the apprentices whom they train, or, finally, their desire to play a less demanding part within the educational system.

When I think about the ideal atmosphere for such research, I think of Columbia University in the fifties, when all of us, both staff and students, took part in various mutually dependent and mutually rewarding enterprises, wherein no one knew precisely who had had the first idea and who should take the credit, or the blame, but no one really cared. The most important issue was the specific problem to be solved, not the one who solved it. The satisfaction that we took from each solution, or each part of a solution, was enough to keep us going day and night. I couldn't wish a better climate for research in 2050.

Introduction to
Howard H. Kendler

In introducing Professor Howard Kendler let me give you a few biographical details and then some personal comments. The first important influence on Howard's professional life was the Gestalt psychologist Solomon Asch, whom Howard had as an undergraduate teacher in Brooklyn College. Asch kindled Howard's interest in experimental psychology and in the specific area of problem solving, on which, judging from later events, he became imprinted. Partly because of his interest in Gestalt psychology and partly because tuition was only $50 a semester, Howard went to Iowa State University for his graduate education. Largely due to a chance encounter, however, he came under the apprenticeship of Kenneth Spence rather than of Kurt Lewin, who was on the faculty at the time. By 1943 Howard had earned his Ph.D. in experimental psychology with a minor in clinical psychology, and had acquired a wife and collaborator, Tracy, who also did her doctoral work with Spence.

These were the war years and Howard, whose poor eyesight excluded him for a time, was inducted into the Army as a private. In spite of, or perhaps because of, his Ph.D. and his severe nearsightedness, he was selected to be trained as a heavy machine gunner. Fortunately for the war effort, the error was eventually discovered, and after receiving a commission and some special training, Howard was assigned to Walter Reed General Hospital. There he practiced clinical psychology until the end of the war.

A 2-year stint as assistant professor at the University of Colorado then began, followed by some 15 years at New York University, where he quickly rose to the rank of Full Professor. In 1963 NYU lost him to his present affiliation, the University of California at Santa Barbara.

Professional recognition came early owing to his incisive work on some of the hot issues of the time—latent learning, drive interaction, and the selective role of drive stimuli in learning. This was all rat research, but in the 50's he returned to his early interest in problem solving and began what was fated to be the dominant research direction of his career. For almost 30 years Howard, in collaboration with his wife, has been concerned with specifying in some precision the emergence of inferential and conceptual behavior in children; how children make the transition from rat-like to human behavior. Characteristically, the work, careful and systematic, is a blend of empirical, theoretical, and methodological analyses.

Theoretical and methodological matters have always been of deep concern to Howard. In fact, about 30% of his more than 100 publications are devoted to these issues, culminating in his penetrating recent book entitled, *Psychology: A Science in Conflict*. A somewhat related work that examines the historical foundations of modern psychology is well under way.

It was in his highly popular "201" course, devoted to methodological analysis, that I, a green but eager graduate student, first met Howard. The course was illuminating and inspiring, full of ideas and controversy. I had been somewhat disenchanted by what then passed as experimental psychology at the downtown campus of New York University, which for the most part consisted of calibrating Dodge tachistocopes, a rather primitive guillotine-type device, applying smoke to drum paper, and the like. So when the opportunity arose, I switched my teaching assistantship to the uptown campus, where Howard was chairman, soon immersing myself in his rat lab. The fact that the stipend for a downtown TA was $800 a year while an uptown TA earned $1000 for the same work had almost nothing to do with my decision.

Some 30 years have passed since that time and, understandably, many details and specific episodes are lost from memory. What will never fade, however, is the recollection that those were intellectually rewarding years, years of hard work lightened by bright companions, optimism for the future and, above all, by a wise and kind advisor.

M. R. D'Amato

3 Retrospections, Contemplations, and Anticipations

Howard H. Kendler
University of California, Santa Barbara

If I could relive my life as a psychologist, I would behave differently. This is neither a confession of regrets nor an admission of errors. I view my career in psychology, which I hasten to add is not over, in an exceedingly tolerant and understanding light. My admission that a second chance for a career in psychology would be guided by a different strategy stems from the belief that my understanding of psychology—its history, its methodology, its theories—has increased immeasurably over the years (Kendler, 1981). Therefore I have become sensitive to issues about which I was initially unclear or unaware. The remainder of this paper seeks to justify this claim.

Probably my most important early intellectual experience lay in the study of geometry in junior high school. Being able to prove relationships among geometrical figures by deductive reasoning created a sense of understanding that served as a model for my subsequent attempts to comprehend empirical phenomena. The imprinting for deductive explanation expanded later on, after reading Darwin, to include nonmathematical forms. In fact, I ultimately became sympathetic to the strategy that, in the attempt to formulate general psychological theories, it would be wiser to emulate Darwin rather than Galileo or Newton.

The decision to become a psychologist was encouraged by my good fortune in enrolling in an undergraduate experimental psychology of thinking class with Solomon E. Asch at Brooklyn College.

Asch had received his doctorate at Columbia University in 1932 and, like many of the bright young psychologists in the New York City area, came under the influence of Max Wertheimer, the founder of Gestalt psychology who had fled from Nazi Germany and become a professor at the New School of Social Research in New York City. An experimental problem in the area of thinking that intrigued Wertheimer was known as the *einstellung* problem, the tendency of mental sets to persist even when they encourage stupid behavior (Luchins, 1942). For example, after learning to solve a sequence of similar arithemetical problems in a set way, I found that many college students confronted with the task of obtaining 5 pints of water with 10, 25, and 5 pint containers solved the problem with a $25 - 10 - 5 - 5 = 5$ sequence. Some who thought themselves clever, used the $10 - 5 = 5$ method. Only a minority solved the problem by directly filling the 5-pint container.

How important is this demonstration of the einstellung phenomenon (mental set)? Both Wertheimer and Asch thought that mental sets reflect the corrupting influence of mechanical habits on problem solving behavior. They laid the blame for such stupid behavior on the drill method that associationistic psychologists, like Edward L. Thorndike, encouraged in elementary schools. I could not share these strong conclusions; habitual modes of behavior can be effective in dealing with the routines of life. Nevertheless I thought the einstellung phenomenon to be interesting and proposed a study designed to test the strength of the set over time. I had formulated a hypothesis that "tension systems" underlying mental sets increased with time. The deductive consequence of this counter-intuitive assumption was that the set would become more powerful with the passage of time. Professor Asch supplied me with the necessary encouragement and cooperation to test my hypothesis. Collecting the data, analyzing, and interpreting the results, proved to be a "peak experience" in the words of Abraham Maslow, for whom I incidentally served as an assistant at Brooklyn College. That my prediction was disconfirmed did not faze me. I actually took pride in the fact that my hypothesis was capable of being falsified, a characteristic not shared by many psychological hypotheses about which I was learning. Only later did I come across Clark Hull's statement, which clearly articulated a strategy toward which I was groping; "It is believed that a clear formulation, even if later found incorrect, will ultimately lead more quickly and easily to a correct formulation than will a pussyfooting statement which might be more difficult to convict a falsity" (Hull, 1943, p. 398).

Professor Asch's encouragement and a romantic attachment to a classmate in my psychology courses led the classmate and myself to graduate school at the University of Iowa where we planned to study with Kurt Lewin who was extending a Gestalt orientation into the fields of personality and social psychology. It soon became apparent that I resonated more to the approach of a young neobehaviorist, Kenneth W. Spence, than I did to the efforts of Kurt Lewin. I did not fully appreciate at that time that the difference between Gestalt Psychology and American Behaviorism lay not only in the primary theoretical assumptions but extended to the subject matter of psychology, the criterion of truth, and the role of psychology in society (Kendler, 1981). The puzzlement generated by the methodological differences between Gestalt psychology and behaviorism, plus a stint as a clinical psychologist during World War II, encouraged a life-long interest in the philosophy of science, that focused on issues directly relevant to my efforts as an empiricist and theorist.

My apprenticeship with Kenneth Spence proved to be productive and rewarding. He frankly admitted to the mission of converting students with Gestalt learnings to Hullian neobehaviorism. I resonated to Spence's approach with its strong and intimate relationship between theory and research and its heavy emphasis on objectivity. I was anxious to get involved in research and after several tough negotiating sessions with Spence I "decided" to do three small studies for my master's thesis; one that he wanted me to do, one that I wanted to do, and one we both agreed should be done. They were all related to the latent learning controversy that became the dominant issue in learning theory after World War II.

In retrospect I question whether most of the participants in that controversy fully appreciated all the issues. The controversy appeared to be between two theories of learning: Tolman's cognitive formulation (1932) and the Hull-Spence (Hull, 1943; Spence, 1956) conception. According to Tolman's view rats learn a cognitive map of mazes without benefit of reward while the Hull-Spence conception was that rats learned stimulus-response association as a consequence of some reinforcement process. The major argument offered in favor of Tolman's view were the California latent learning studies (Blodgett, 1929; Tolman & Honzik, 1930) in which rats who received no food reward in the end-box of a multi-unit maze learned as much about the structure of the maze as rats who were rewarded with food, a finding that was embarrassing to a formulation that learning was dependent on some reinforcement process. The counter argument of the Hull-Spence theory was based on irrelevant-incentive studies in a T-maze, which found that rats could not learn the location of food or water if they did not consume it (Spence & Lippitt, 1946; Kendler, 1947), a finding directly in opposition to a prediction made by cognitive theory (Tolman, 1934; Spence & Kendler, 1948) that rats, through experience alone, learn the structure of their environment.

The latent learning controversy, which occupied the efforts of hundreds of researchers, and the interests of thousands, developed through four stages. First there was the *combatant stage* in which two major theories presumably stood in direct opposition to each other. The second stage was one of *"critical experiments"* in which the results of numerous studies, some ingeniously designed (e.g., Kendler & Mencher, 1948; Kanner, 1954), were offered to reveal the fundamental inadequacy of the opposing theory. The *confusion stage* followed in which large amounts of data overwhelmed the explanatory capacity of each theory. Theoretical ambiguities, failures to replicate basic findings, a patchwork of ad hoc theorizing, a desire to win the controversy at the expense of understanding the phenomena, all contributed to a state of confusion from which the controversy never recovered. The final stage, *disenchantment,* led to the gradual abandonment of the controversy without any satisfactory resolution. Some representatives of each side claimed victory in a manner analogous to Senator Aiken's recommendation that United States acknowledged their victory in the Vietnam War by withdrawing its troops. My reaction to the controversy was expressed in the 1959 Annual Review article on Learning:

> It appeared to many, a decade ago, that certain theories notably those of Hull and Tolman, were engaged in mortal combat in the arena of hard data. Now that the dust has settled, it seems that the combatants were more often shadow boxing. Damage to the theoretical positions did occur but in many instances the wounds were self-inflicted. However, these theoretical disputes nevertheless did serve a purpose. They provided much interesting data; but more important they revealed the stark inadequacies and limitations of existing learning theories (Kendler, 1959, p. 43).

If victory and defeat were to be assigned, the verdict would have to be that both Tolman's cognitive theory and the Hull-Spence neobehavioristic formulation lost. Their conceptions, in spite of valiant attempts at ad hoc theorizing, proved incapable of interpreting all the latent learning phenomena in a rigorous manner. Victory was achieved indirectly by Estes' mathematical modeling of learning phenomena and Skinner's atheoretical operant approach. Estes, an admirer of the Hull-Spence theoretical attempts, concluded that their mathematical efforts were inadequate. More rigorous stochastic models (Estes, 1959) were needed to eliminate the deductive ambiguities of the general learning theories of Tolman and Hull-Spence. Skinner's victory stemmed from his rejection of abstract theorizing in favor of an atheoretical description of what he considered to be basic learning phenomena. In essence Estes and Skinner achieved victories by proposing solutions, admittedly different, to the failures of the Tolman and Hull-Spence systems. From the perspective of history, the latent learning controversy exerted an impact similar to the imageless thought controversy during the early part of the twentieth century (Woodworth, 1938). The inability to resolve that controversy not only led to its abandonment but also to the rejection of the introspective mode of psychological investigation. Similarly, the latent learning controversy led to the rejection of the empirical problem at issue as well as the ultimate goal of formulating a general learning theory. I would suggest that both controversies dealt with important empirical problems but the methods used were inadequate to their tasks.

The common interpretation, which I accepted, was that the Tolman and Hull-Spence conceptions were too imprecise to cope with the empirical issues in the controversy. The solution was to make such theories more precise. But this strategy failed. Mathematical models of learning which initially aspired to generality (e.g., Estes & Burke, 1953) discovered that their precision could only be achieved by severely restricting their empirical implications. Many such models proved to be more of a formal exercise than a serious attempt at theorizing.

While engaged in theoretical issues of animal learning I was approached by government agencies to do research in human problem solving. In blunt terms I was being seduced by research money. I yielded. I was soon confronted with a fundamental question that is too often superficially treated. What strategy should I adopt for my new research program? What hypotheses should be tested, what research design should be used, and what subjects should be employed? Problems of strategy, in those days, did not appear to be of paramount interest because of the prevailing optimistic view that a research strategy need only be heuristic; it can be justified by the research it stimulates. William James had previously rationalized such a view by his assertion that, "Facts are facts and if we get enough of them they are sure to combine." Our history refutes James's optimism and challenges the notion that research programs can be justified by their heuristic value. Psychology is burdened with a scrap heap of empirical results which have contributed nothing to our field except to increase the number of publications and to justify academic promotions. The trouble with this harsh criticism is that it fails to suggest a remedy. How can fruitful research be guaranteed? It cannot. No recipe can be formulated that would automatically ensure important results. But this does not deny the possibility that some guidelines might help to increase the probability of significant research.

I must confess that the issue of strategy did not dominate my thinking when I planned research in problem solving. I thought that a reasonable plan would be to investigate the influence of variables and processes known to be important in simple associative learning in order to see how they influenced problem solving. One study revealed that variables that facilitated experimental extinction operated to overcome a mental set (Kendler, Greenberg, & Richman, 1952). Another study (Kendler & Vineberg, 1954) found that the acquisition of conjunctive concepts was facilitated by the previous learning of the affirmative concepts of which the conjunctive concept was composed. The significant results obtained, however, did not convince me that my research problems were significant. I had the uneasy feeling that my research was generated more by the availability of researchable problems than by a compelling research strategy.

This insecurity was eased after I came across an experimental paradigm (Buss, 1953) that seems to have important empirical and theoretical implications. The experimental design involved two successive discrimination tasks which required the second task to be solved in a different way from the first one. In a reversal shift the subject was required to reverse its preference; if in the initial task a black stimulus, regardless of its size, was positive, then in the postshift discrimination, the white stimulus, regardless of its size, would become positive. In an extradimensional shift, the subject was required to shift from a value of one dimension to a value of another dimension (e.g., from *black* to *large*).

This discrimination-shift design appeared to be empirically sig-nificant because evidence from my laboratory (Kelleher, 1956; Ken-dler & D'Amato, 1956) indicated that rats could execute an extradimensional shift more rapidly than a reversal shift while adult humans behaved in the opposite manner, finding a reversal shift easier. That is, a "psychological gap" separated the rat from the adult human in discrimination-shift behavior. Filling in that gap would presumably have important comparative and developmental implica-tions.

The reversal-extradimensional comparison was important the-oretically because Spence's discrimination-learning model, based upon stimulus-response conditioning principles, predicted an extra-dimensional shift should be easier than a reversal shift (H. H. Ken-dler, Hirschberg, & Wolford, 1952). How should one view a theory that predicts the behavior of rats, but not of human beings?

A Darwinian framework, would discourage the view that a sharp qualitative difference separates the rat from humans. One would expect continuities as well as discontinuities especially when one remembers, which at times is difficult, that infants and children are human. Thus I was encouraged to perceive the discrepancy between the behavior of rats and adult humans as reflecting both quantitative and qualitative changes.

In order to discover the nature of the psychological gap between rats and adult humans a tentative and provisional theory of discrimi-nation-shift behavior was proposed to guide the research program. The theory consisted of two related models. One, to account for the behavior of rats, was essentially Spence's single-unit model, which postulates that a stimulus becomes directly associated, in a figurative sense, to a response. The second, a mediational stimulus-response model, formulated to account for adult human behavior, postulated a chain of two stimulus response associations in which the initial response was an implicit *representation* of the relevant dimension (e.g., brightness). It was assumed that this mediated representational response could be employed in a reversal shift but had to be discarded in an extradimensional shift and hence the reversal shift would be easier to execute. An important difference should be noted between my proposed mediated chain and Watson's (1919) famous chain of sensory-motor reflexes. I postulated that implicit responses could vary in abstract representational functioning whereas hierarchical representation was omitted from Watson's formulation. Rats, in my conception, were assumed to make a common response to the specific stimuli (e.g., black and white) while adult humans were assumed to respond to conceptual properties (e.g., brightness).

My wife, Tracy Kendler, joined me in this research program and brought to it, among other abilities, a sophistication in developmental psychology which I lacked. Being research colleagues proved to be a test of our marriage; we soon learned that differing methodological and theoretical views created greater problems than the conventional marital conflicts. It became customary when lecturing about our research program to always add the proviso that one's views does not necessarily represent those of the other. I now add such a proviso.

As noted, our research program operated under a Darwinian bias, perhaps as much by tradition as by strategic choice. In retrospect I ask myself why I indulged in abstract theorizing instead of attempting to relate my theoretical assumptions to underlying neurophysiological processes. Several factors operated, some of which were obviously tangential to the basic issue. An undergraduate biology course turned me off because of the instructor's desire to integrate biological phenomena with Marxist-Leninist principles, an attempt that in my estimation, corrupted biology with irrelevant metaphysical issues. Limited training and reading in physiological psychology failed to inspire the intellectual excitement that was generated by the broad and abstract theoretical conceptions of Hull and Spence, and Tolman. I also became suspicious of broad neurophysiological speculations about complex phenomena that lacked predictive powers while simultaneously promoting a false sense of understanding. Perhaps my main justification for approaching our research program within a "black-box" orientation was my strategic conviction that research problems first had to be "structured" in order to highlight basic theoretical issues. Only then would a finer-grain neurophysiological analysis be productive.

Our attempt to fill in the gap between the discrimination shift behavior of rats and adults humans started with a study with kindergarten children. As a group, kindergarteners executed a reversal and extradimensional shift at approximately the same rate suggesting "that the point in human development was discovered which was psychologically halfway between the white rat and college student" (H. H. Kendler & Kendler, 1962). The data gave strong support to the idea that we had discovered a transitional stage of development in which some of the children were responding to a single-unit manner, like rats, and the remainder were operating in a mediational representational fashion, like college students. To clarify developmental changes it became necessary to devise a new method that would measure the tendency of an individual subject to respond in a reversal manner. Data gathered with this new optional discrimination-shift technique (T. S. Kendler, Kendler, & Silfen, 1964; T. S. Kendler, Kendler, & Learnard, 1962) demonstrated that rat behavior is consistent with the simple associative model based on conditioning principles whereas the behavior of college students is consistent with the mediational model that postulates that the subject processes the discriminanda conceptually and this representation guides subsequent behavior. The probability that a child's behavior will fit the single-unit or mediational mode depends on age; the younger the child the more likely the behavior will be controlled by single-unit processes whereas the older the child the more likely it is that mediational mechanisms will take over.

Our plan after demonstrating ontogenetic changes in discrimination-shift behavior, was to make a more detailed analysis of the mediational process. An obstacle to this plan arose from unanticipated criticisms. Tracy suggested that we should "turn the other cheek" to our critics and go about our work. I, being a combative New Yorker, assigned a different anatomical meaning to her recommendation and therefore felt compelled to rebut the criticisms. Admittedly some time was wasted in these efforts (H. H. Kendler & Kendler, 1966; 1969; 1971) but I would maintain that important methodological and theoretical issues were clarified.

One reason we attracted criticism was that our experimental procedures were relatively simple to execute. The demand for "quickie" research to meet the requirements for a thesis or publication, or both, could easily be met by testing some simple-minded hypothesis with our simple research technique. One favorite gambit was to test the assumption, falsely attributed to us, that the day before their fifth birthday children went to bed as simple associative creatures and woke up as mediators. Any data that failed to agree with this hypothesis would be interpreted as disproving our developmental theory. Our theory predicted orderly developmental changes, not a specific reaction at a given age level regardless of the discriminada used. Another favorite gambit was to compare the discrimination-shift behavior of two closely related age groups with a small number of subjects in each group. Failure to find a significant difference was interpreted as disproving our theory, which was based on ontogenetic studies involving a wide age range with large numbers of subjects in each of several age groups. Another thorn in our sides was the labeling of our theory as a "verbal mediation" conception in spite of our repeated insistence this was not the case. In our initial theoretical paper (H. H. Kendler & Kendler, 1962) we explicitly stated, "It would be unwise and strategically shortsighted to *identify* mediational events with introspective reports or language behavior, or other observable events" (H. H. Kendler & Kendler, 1962, p. 7). Aside from its representational function we left the mediational process open-ended so that its structural properties and operating characteristics could be revealed by further research. Unfortunately, our repeated efforts to clarify this theoretical issue failed because the public interpretation of a theory appears to depend more on its critics than its authors.

Legitimate criticisms of our developmental theory came mainly from two sources; both husband and wife research teams. My clinical intuition, in which I have great confidence, has never satisfactorily explained why discrimination-shift behavior should have special fascination for psychologists who are married to each other. Perhaps I resist knowing the truth. The Zeamans (House & Zeaman, 1963) offered an *observing response* interpretation, which denied ontogenetic changes, while the Tighes (T. J. Tighe & Tighe, 1966), accepting the validity of developmental changes, explained them within a *perceptual differentiation* model. I am convinced that if the discrimination-shift controversy is re-examined from today's vantage point, an unbiased, fair-minded, intelligent critic would conclude that we were basically correct about the validity of developmental changes and the essential role played by representational functioning. This claim does not deny that attentional and perceptual factors can influence discrimination-shift behavior; only that conceptual processes are basic.

In order to pin down the conceptual basis of developmental changes in discrimination-shift behavior, a series of studies (H. H. Kendler & Kendler, 1975) was conducted with a wide variety of discriminada—nonsense syllables, unrelated words, conceptually related words, conceptually related pictures—all of which produced results consistent with the hypothesis that changes in representational functioning were responsible for observed ontogenetic changes. Such results could not be explained on the basis of perceptual processes unless the perceptual mechanism was expanded to include representational functioning. At the same time we were attacking the theoretical assumptions of our major critics, we began extending our dual stage theory by investigating the transition between single-unit and mediational functioning and by proposing a more detailed analysis of the encoding mechanisms. One important set of findings (H. H. Kendler, Kendler, & Marken, 1969; T. S. Kendler, 1971) demonstrated that a variety of conditions could produce a mediational deficiency in adult humans so that their behavior would be controlled by simple associative mechanisms. In addition, our theoretical model extended its empirical range by predicting results in the fields of memory (H. H. Kendler, Kendler, & Marken, 1970; Kendler & Ward, 1971) and conceptual development (H. H. Kendler & Guenther, 1980). Finally, Tracy Kendler (1979) has reformulated and extended the dual-stage model into a larger empirical realm by proposing a level-of-processing model that is guided by neurological evidence.

How is our research program to be evaluated? Thomas Leahey (1980), an historian who admits to admiring "Piaget, Tolman, and Chomsky, more than . . . Watson, Hull and Skinner," evaluates our efforts within a Kuhnian (Kuhn, 1961) historical conception: "The Kendlers' analysis of discrimination shift learning is an example of a paradigm successfully responding to anomalous findings." That is, the discrimination-shift behavior of adult humans was inconsistent with the principles of the Hull-Spence conditioning model and our efforts were successful in interpreting these and other results within an expanded version of the Hull-Spence formulation. If one adopts the Kuhnian view of the history of science which postulates a repetitive historical cycle composed of two markedly different enterprises, normal science and revolution, then I concur with Leahey's conclusion. However, a Kuhnian view of the history of psychology is, at best, incomplete and at worst, distorted. "Historical discontinuities are emphasized at the expense of continuities" (Kendler, in press), and tides of thought which engulf an entire discipline, rather than a specific paradigm, are ignored. Our research program, in addition to its specific neobehavioristic implications, contributed to three important evolutionary trends occurring during the past few decades: (1) a rising disenchantment with general theories of behavior that are based upon a single model of behavior, (2) a gradual realization that black-box theories are incapable of resolving basic theoretical differences, and (3) the necessity of expanding theoretical processes to account for human cognitive behavior.

1.   Our dual-process, developmental formulation shares characteristics with numerous attempts in the past to explain behavior on the basis of two distinct types of models: Pavlov's (1955) first and second-signal system, Carr's (1925) motor and rational method of problem solving, Piaget's (1952) sensorimotor versus thought processes distinction, Hebb's (1966) division between sense-dominated and mediated processes, and even with Freud's distinction between primary and secondary processes. This concurrence of opinion offers reassurance about the validity of our distinction between associationistic and mediational (cognitive) models of behavior. By accepting the validity of this distinction, it becomes important to develop flexible and exacting experimental paradigms, like our discrimination-shift procedure, to study ontogenetic and phylogenetic factors underlying different models of behavior.

2.   Although I was confident about the general validity of our theoretical hypotheses, it gradually became apparent that an unqualified resolution of the controversy with our critics would not be forthcoming. The sequence of events bore an uncomfortable similarity to those that occurred in the latent learning controversy. A combatant stage, triggered by the criticism of our two-stage formulation, encouraged a stage of "critical experiments" which produced a stage of confusion that ultimately led, for most participants, to a disenchantment with the entire controversy. One could easily attribute this failure to the lack of precision in the competing theories, a viewpoint that, you may recall, I adopted when trying to explain the failure of the latent learning controversy to yield a clear-cut resolution. Another possibility should be considered. Perhaps black-box theorizing, formulations that employ abstract theoretical constructs, have limited explanatory powers:

> Black-box theories . . . have been plagued by persistent and unresolvable theoretical disputes. . . . One of the main reasons that these theoretical disputes go unresolved is that black-box theories do not provide sufficient constraints to allow for resolutions of theoretical disputes. The environmental operations are too far removed from the underlying biological mechanisms that are responsible for behavior. As a consequence numerous theoretical options are available to handle embarrassing data. The result is that core assumptions of black-box

theories are able to survive regardless of what results are obtained, thus effectively preventing one theory from achieving dominance over its competitors. In contrast, physiological theories that identify the operation of permanent structures or biochemical reactions are being responsible for given forms of behavior have relatively fewer options in defending their truth value when predictions fail (Kendler, 1981, pp. 124–125).

Don't misunderstand me! I am not denying the instrumental value of black-box theories. Nor am I guaranteeing the success of neuropsychological formulations. I am only suggesting that a large measure of theoretical ambiguity resides in black box formulations that can be markedly reduced if the implications of the formulation can be recast into neurophysiological operations.

3. Our dual-stage developmental research program had the effect, along with the efforts of others (e.g., Osgood, C. E., 1957), of expanding the empirical realm of neobehaviorism, in our case from discrimination learning to cognitive development. Our efforts began a few years before the cognitive revolution (Neisser, 1967) erupted. There were points of similarity between our neobehavioristic conception and the initial cognitive models: A simple stimulus-response analysis was insufficient for problem-solving behavior, representation was a basic function in cognitive behavior, and fundamental behavioral events were generated "within the organism" as contrasted with being evoked by external stimulation. At the same time differences prevailed. We accepted a stimulus-response language (H. H. Kendler, 1965), enlarged by additional constructs, as a convenient idiom to represent psychological events, we abjured mentalistic concepts because of the false sense of understanding they encourage, and we maintained a Darwinian orientation.

The similarities, and even some of the differences, were ignored because cognitive psychologists emphasized revolutionary notions at the expense of evolutionary changes. Perhaps this is necessary to gain the enthusiasm and dedication required to launch a new paradigm. But a price is paid for an evangelical fervor that blots out the lessons of the past. Santayana warns us, "Those who cannot remember the past are condemned to repeat it." The history of psychology has suggested that sheer amassing of data will not automatically create progress, that black-box theories suffer from a fatal ambiguity, that biological structures underlying the actions of organisms should not be ignored, and that intuitive understanding is no substitute for theoretical deductions. Only by profiting from the lessons of history will cognitive psychology avoid the fate of those revolutionary paradigms of the past whose early successes, in time, turned into delayed failures.

A radical redirection must now take place in my discussion in my speculations about psychology's future are to be completed. Up to now, my projections have been limited to problems of research and theory. The progress that psychology will make, however, will not alone be determined by the success psychologists achieve in these areas. Of tremendous importance to psychology's future wil be society's perception and acceptance of psychology's social role.

Too many psychologists, in my estimation, either are ignorant of, or refuse to take seriously, the intrinsic disunity of psychology. Psychologists disagree markedly among themselves about the appropriate subject matter of psychology, the criterion of psychological "truth," and the social responsibilities of psychologists. These issues are exceedingly complex and require subtle analyses for clarification. Since I have attempted that task elsewhere (Kendler, 1981) I feel justified in now expressing bold, sweeping opinions to complete my talk within my alotted time.

One of the basic divisions within psychology concerns the proper conceptualization of the discipline: whether psychology is a natural science that employs those procedures that have yielded reliable knowledge in the physical and biological sciences, or whether psychology is a human science that can with the assistance of phenomenological insights reveal the essence of the human condition and discover "valid" moral principles that should guide human conduct.

It should surprise nobody that my *decision* is to view psychology as a natural science. The implication of this choice is that psychologists should recognize the epistemological principle that facts and values are logically dissociated and consequently psychologists cannot *prescribe* to society a set of ethical imperatives. We can, however, serve the needs of a democratic society, as John Dewey (1900) noted many years ago, by *describing* the empirical consequences of different moral choices and social policies so that society can rationally choose among them.

Unfortunately these irreconcilable orientations—natural science vs. human science—cannot be treated simply as a philosophical disagreement. Psychology is being, and will continue to be, judged by society. The encouragement and support that psychology will receive will be dependent on that judgment. It is my conviction that psychology's future will be hampered if psychology is perceived as a form of moral dictation or political action. Richard Atkinson (1977) expresses this position more strongly, "To permit psychology to be misused as an advocate of public policy will lead inevitably to the demise of the field." A democratic society should be suspicious of those who are convinced that they alone know what is right and what is good—whether they be religious zealots, political fanatics, or theoretical psychologists.

We psychologists who aspire to the noble goal of a natural-science psychology face a protracted struggle to overcome great obstacles. We have to profit from the lessons of the past so that our research and theoretical efforts can be improved. We have to make clear to the society in which we live our scientific goal and social role. Eventual success can only be achieved by intellectual creativity and dedication to the ideals of natural science.

REFERENCES

Atkinson, R. C. Reflections on psychology's past and concerns about its future. *American Psychologist*, 1977, *32*, 205–210.

Blodgett, H. C. The effect of the introduction of reward upon the maze performance of rats. *University of California Publications in Psychology*, 1929, *4*, 113–134.

Buss, A. H. Rigidity as a function of reversal and nonreversal shifts in the learning of successive discriminations. *Journal of Experimental Psychology*, 1956, *52*, 162–166.

Carr, H. A. *Psychology: A study of mental activity.* New York: Lonemans, Green and Co., 1925.

Dewey, J. Psychology and social practice. *Psychological Review*, 1900, *7*, 105–124.

Estes, W. K., & Burke, C. J. A theory of stimulus variability in learning. *Psychological Review*, 1953, *60*, 276–286.

Hebb, D. O. *The textbook of psychology* (2nd ed.) Philadelphia: Saunders, 1960.

Hull, C. L. *Principles of behavior.* New York: Appleton-Century, 1943.

Kanner, J. H. A test of whether the "nonrewarded" animals learned as much as the "rewarded" animals in the California latent learning study. *Journal of Experimental Psychology*, 1954, *48*, 175–183.

Kelleher, R. T. Discrimination learning as a function of reversal and nonreversal shifts. *Journal of Experimental Psychology*, 1956, *61*, 379–384.

Kendler, H. H. An investigation of latent learning in a T-maze. *Journal of Comparative and Physiological Psychology*, 1947, *40*, 265–270.

Kendler, H. H. Learning. In P. R. Farnsworth & Q. McNemar (Eds.) *Annual review of psychology*. Annual Reviews: Stanford, California, 1959.

Kendler, H. H. Motivation and behavior. In D. Levine (Ed.) *Nebraska symposium on motivation*. Lincoln, Nebraska: University of Nebraska Press, 1965.

Kendler, H. H. *Psychology: A science in conflict*. New York: Oxford, 1981.

Kendler, H. H. Evolution or revolutions (To appear in a book edited by K. Lagerspetz & P. Niemi).

Kendler, H. H. & D'Amato, M. F. A comparison of reversal shifts and nonreversal shifts in human concept formation behavior. *Journal of Experimental Psychology*, 1955, *49*, 165–174.

Kendler, H. H., Greenberg, A., & Richman, H. The influence of massed and distributed practice on the development of mental set. *Journal of Experimental Psychology*, 1952, *43*, 21–25.

Kendler, H. H. & Guenther, K. Developmental changes in classificatory behavior. *Child Development*, 1980, *51*, 339–348.

Kendler, H. H., Hirschberg, M. A., & Wolford, G. Spence's prediction about reversal-shift behavior. *Psychological Review*, 1971, *78*, 4, 354.

Kendler, H. H. & Kendler, T. S. Vertical and horizontal processes in problem solving. *Psychological Review*, 1962, *69*, 1–16.

Kendler, H. H. & Kendler, T. S. Selective attention vs. mediation: Some comments on Mackintosh's analysis of two-stage models of discrimination learning. *Psychological Bulletin*, 1966, *66*, 272–280.

Kendler, H. H. & Kendler, T. S. Reversal shift behavior: Some basic issues. *Psychological Bulletin*, 1969, *72*, 229–232.·

Kendler, H. H. & Kendler, T. S. Definitely, our last word! *Psychological Bulletin*, 1971, *75*, 290–293.

Kendler, H. H. & Mencher, H. C. The ability of rats to learn the location of food when motivated by thirst—An experimental reply to Leeper. *Journal of Experimental Psychology*, 1948, *38*, 82–88.

Kendler, H. H. & Vineberg, R. The acquisition of compound concepts as a function of previous training. *Journal of Experimental Psychology*, 1954, *48*, 282–285.

Kendler, H. H. & Ward, J. W. Memory loss following discrimination of conceptually related material. *Journal of Experimental Psychology*, 1971, *88*, 435–436.

Kendler, H. H. & Ward, J. W. Recognition and recall of related and unrelated words. *Psychonomic Science*, 1972, *28*, 346–348.

Kendler, T. S. From early to later learning. In M. E. Meyer (Ed.) *Second Western Symposium on learning: Early learning*. Bellingham, Washington: Western Washington State College, 1971.

Kendler, T. S. The development of discrimination learning: A levels-of-functioning explanation. In H. W. Reese & L. P. Lipsitt (Eds.) *Advances in child development and behavior. Volume 13*. New York: Academic Press, 1979.

Kendler, T. S., Kendler, H. H., & Learnard, B. Mediated responses to size and brightness as a function of age. *American Journal of Psychology*, 1962, *75*, 571–586.

Kendler, T. S., Kendler, H. H. & Silfen, C. K. Optional shift behavior of albino rats. *Psychonomic Science*, 1964, *1*, 5–6.

Kuhn, T. S. *The structure of scientific revolutions*. Chicago: University of Chicago Press, 1962.

Leahey, T. H. *A history of psychology*. Englewood Cliffs, New Jersey: Prentice-Hall, 1980.

Luchins, A. S. Mechanization in problem solving. *Psychological Monographs*, 1942, *54*, (6), Whole No. 248.

Neisser, U. *Cognitive psychology*. New York: Appleton-Century-Crofts, 1967.

Osgood, C. E. A behavioristic analysis of perception and language as cognitive phenomena. *Contemporary approaches to cognition: A symposium held at the University of Colorado*. Cambridge, Massachusetts: Harvard University Press, 1957.

Pavlov, I. P. Selected works. Moscow, USSR: Langley Publishing, 1955 (Trans. by S. Belsky).

Piaget, J. The origins of intelligence in children. New York: International University Press, 1952.

Spence, K. W. *Behavior theory and conditioning*. New Haven: Yale University Press, 1956.

Spence, K. W. & Kendler, H. H. The speculations of Leeper with respect to the Iowa tests of the Sign-Gestalt theory of learning. *Journal of Experimental Psychology*, 1948, *38*, 106–109.

Spence, K. W. & Lippitt, R. An experimental test of the Sign-Gestalt theory of trial and error learning. *Journal of Experimental Psychology*, 1946, *36*, 491–502.

Tolman, E. C. *Purposive behavior in animals and men*. New York: Century, 1932.

Tolman, E. C. Theories of learning. Chapter XII in Moss, F. A. (Ed.) *Comparative Psychology*, New York: Prentice-Hall, 1934.

Tolman, E. C., & Houzik, C. H. Introduction and removal of reward and maze performance of rats. *University of California Publications in Psychology*, 1930, *4*, 257–275.

Watson, J. B. *Psychology from the standpoint of a behaviorist*. Philadelphia, PA: Lippincott, 1919.

Woodworth, R. S. *Experimental Psychology*. New York: Holt, 1938.

Introduction to
Karl H. Pribram

Dr. Pribram received his bachelor of science and medical degrees from the University of Chicago. Following a residency at St. Luke's hospital, he became an instructor in surgery at the University of Tennessee. From there he moved on to the Yerkes Primate laboratory as a neurophysiologist while concurrently opening a private practice in neurology and neurosurgery in Florida. In 1948 he moved on to Yale Universtiy where he held appointments in the departments of Psychiatry and Psychology. From 1951 to 1958 he was also director of the Institute for Living in Hartford. Since 1959 he had been at Stanford in the departments of Psychology and Psychiatry and he is Head of the Neuropsychology Laboratories at Stanford. In 1962 he was given a lifetime research award by the National Institutes of Health.

The scope and magnitude of Dr. Pribram's interests and research have been truly remarkable. He has served on the editorial board of journals as diverse as *Human Motivation, Neuroscience Research, Journal of Autism and Developmental Disorders, Journal of Mental Imagery, Cognition and Personality, Journal of Mathematical Biology,* and the *Journal of Human Movement Studies.*

He has published over 150 review and theoretical papers, well over 100 research papers, 13 books and monographs, and numerous book reviews and commentaries.

His research interests, like his writing, have been diverse and yet there are some central themes that characterize his contributions to science. One of these is the role of cognitive processes in behavior.

In 1960 he was a co-author with George Miller and Eugene Galanter of *Plans and the Structure of Behavior*—a book which critiqued the S-R reflex concept and developed it into an interactionist-feedback model. The book also considered the relationship between thought processes and the functioning of computers—thereby becoming an early contributor to the field of artificial intelligence, and it essentially laid the groundwork for the cognitive revolution that subsequently swept through first human learning research and, more recently, animal learning research.

In 1971 his book *Languages of the Brain* continued the development of the feedback model of behavior, introduced a consideration of the synaptic junction as the locus of neuro-behavioral flexibility (a conjecture now clearly borne out in Eric Kandel's work on habituation in Aplysia), and related the interaction among neural slow potentials that takes place at the synapse to the concepts of holography.

In the popular press Pribram has been described as the Magellan of the Mind and, indeed, in his research he has circumnavigated the cortex from occipital lobe to frontal lobe and back again. He has critiqued the Hubel and Wiesel analysis of visual receptor function—showing that the receptor fields of cortical neurons are not fixed but, instead, may be modified by the nature of the stimulus impinging on them and/or by activity in other parts of the brain—both cortical and subcortical.

He has tackled the 100 year old question of localization of function in the brain and come down squarely on both sides. For example, he has hypothesized that memory storage is distributed—possibly following a holographic model—but that retrieval programs for memory may be localized. That is—memories are *dis*membered during the storage process and *re*membered during the retrieval process.

Karl and his students, and his students' students, have carried on an extensive series of experiments analyzing the function of the amygdala. His experiments have shown that the amygdala is important for the habituation of some, but not all, aspects of the orienting response, and that the amygdala is also important for Pavlovian conditioning. Karl's long research program has also shown that the

Karl Pribram

amygdala functions as an important nodal point in the network controlling the four Fs—fighting, fleeing, feeding, and sex.

Recently he has taken to the analysis of music—extending the Chomskian analysis of music first offered by Leonard Bernstein.

Currently he is working with Bob Isaacson on a third volume of their series on the hippocampus, he is writing nine book chapters, and he and Richard Thompson have recently received a substantial grant from the Navy to continue their analysis of the neural mechanisms of learning and memory.

In all of his research Dr. Pribram has attempted to integrate the work of the physiological psychologists with that of the animal learning people, and the work of the cognitive psychologists with that of the behaviorists; he has attempted to find applications of psychological concepts in other fields and to bring the concepts of other fields into psychology. Finally, he has attempted to bring the exciting work of psychology to the attention of the public at large.

Charles Flaherty

4 Brain, Behavioral Operants, Cognitive Operations, and Holonomic Transformations

Karl H. Pribram

INTRODUCTION

First, let me thank you for your hospitality. Not only has Rutgers arranged a small snowstorm as a cheerful setting for a warm welcome: in addition, a prearrival gift made my flight to New Brunswick memorable. On my seat someone had left a New York Times. On the back page of the front section of this honorable newspaper, a full page advertisement had been placed, ostensibly by Omni Magazine. In part, the ad read as follows:

> In a recent issue, OMNI Magazine discussed the problems of perception and memory with Dr. Karl Pribram, the Austrian-born neuropsychologist who developed the first holographic model of the brain. According to Pribram, the brain encodes information on a three dimensional energy field that enfolds time and space, yet allows us to recall or reconstruct specific images from the countless millions stored in a space slightly smaller than a melon.
>
> The Pribram interview is a rich, provocative example of the journalism that has made OMNI the world's leading science magazine.

Provocative, it certainly is. I was puzzled as to what it might have been that I had said that would make someone, anyone, even the current "media hype," attribute to me such a view of "the" brain. Ah, yes. The fields are the receptive fields of neurons. And true, a two dimensional orthogonal (spectral) transform will enfold a three dimensional space/time image. Storage capacity in the spectral domain is indeed prodigious. Of course, this domain is but one of several of the "languages of the brain," but on the whole, someone had read me better than I had initially read them.

The Omni interview and other similar experiences have made me wonder how is it that my theoretical work has engaged so much popular interest, while discoveries made in the laboratory have so often become part of the received wisdom in the neurosciences without popular fanfare or even acknowledgment within psychology. The laboratory research takes up by far the greatest amount of my time and effort, and I therefore welcome this opportunity to write a brief biography of the research program.

The following report outlines the several phases of the research, the major discoveries, the theoretical work that has stemmed from these discoveries, and lists the doctoral and postdoctoral students and colleagues who integrally forwarded the program. But before such descriptions must come the sources which motivated the initiation of the program, previous investigators on whose shoulders we have stood to look beyond the heritage which they left to us.

ROOTS

This story began in Chicago, which at the time of my medical training in neurological surgery was a major center for brain research. At the University of Chicago, where I received my undergraduate and medical degrees, were Heinrich Kluever and Paul Bucy, pioneers in investigations of the functions of the temporal lobe of the brain. I became Bucy's first resident when he moved to the nearby Chicago Memorial Hospital and wrote up our first one hundred brain operations in order to have the residency accredited. Bucy was editing a volume on the precentral motor cortex at the time and I became privy to the controversies and details of explorations of this research, as well as learning the techniques of surgery from a master.

Stephen Polyak was working on the anatomy of the retina and visual system. I was intrigued by the work of Roaf on color afterimages and saw in Polyak's detailing of three sorts of retinal bipolar cells a mechanism for analyzing and further separating the Helmholtzian receptor process while accounting for the effects of color afterimages. I wrote up these suggestions with Polyak's help and submitted the result as a medical student thesis.

Paul Weiss was training Roger Sperry to transplant limbs of Amblystoma. We became well acquainted when Weiss appeared on my medical service during my internship. The friendship has lasted a lifetime and centered on the problem of "resonance": How could it be that a limb induces in the developing nervous system a code that allows the system to "recognize" the limb irrespective of its innervation. Sperry's answer to this question invoked specific chemical codes; mine, suggested in *Languages of the Brain,* devolves on the finding by J. Z. Young of the induction of specific nerve fiber size spectra by each muscle. Probably both chemistry and fiber size are involved.

A. Earl Walker became chief of Neurological Surgery when Paul Bucy left and from Walker I learned the details of thalamic anatomy before joining Bucy. Also during this period Ward Halstead introduced me to the procedures used to study the effects of brain injury in humans.

The University of Chicago was not the only center for neuroscience research in Chicago at the time. Magoun and Lindsley and their collaborators were beginning their research on the mesencephalic reticular formation at Northwestern University. I was to participate in this work in collaboration with Percival Bailey, having received a fellowship to do so, but Bailey changed his plans and went overseas for that year. The proposed collaboration never took place but my interest in the project had been piqued so that I kept abreast of developments as they occurred.

At the University of Illinois Neuropsychiatric Institute, Eric Oldberg had gathered a stellar group that included Percival Bailey, Gerhrdt von Bonin, and Warren McCulloch. After my year with Bucy, I became Oldberg's resident with priviledged access to this group. Bailey took another resident (John Green) and me and sat with us over a six-month period detailing his methods and neuroembryological approach to his pioneering work on the classification of brain tumors.

I occasionally participated in the strychninization experiments of chimpanzee cortex and listened attentively to Bailey, Bonin, and McCulloch discuss the results. Some years later, at Yale University, I was able to put to good use my surgical skills and the knowledge I had acquired from these discussions to complete these chemical stimulation experiments on cat and monkey by explorations of the medial and basal surfaces of the brain which had remained inaccessible to the earlier research.

But perhaps the most exciting part of the research was the exploration of the lateral surface of the human brain for suppressor activity. Though the results obtained were highly controversial, the process of cortical stimulation in which Bucy also participated, the examination of the patient (sometimes left to me) while this stimulation was in progress, and the discussions which ensued were fascinating. I remember well the occasion during one of these procedures when a telegram arrived from Oxford University which stated that Paul Glees had just found connections from the precentral cortex to the caudate nucleus, using his newly developed silver technique. McCulloch suggested that the term "feedback" be applied to explain what was happening and that Glees had found the anatomical basis for such feedback.

These are only some of the highlights of the Chicago period. There are many, many stories of fascinating encounters, but one will suffice. My first public address was made to the Chicago Neurological Society. I presented a case of an oligodendroglioma of the motor cortex which had produced localized seizures of facial sweating. The tumor was successfully removed with no aftereffects and a cessation of the seizures. Two conclusions were reached: Careful resections of cortical tissue which did not deeply invade white matter did not result in any irreversible paralysis; the precentral motor cortex is involved in the regulation of visceroautonomic functions which, at the time, were thought to be autonomous with respect to cortex with hypothalamic mechanisms as the highest level of control.

The other person on the program was Warren McCulloch. I did not understand a single word of what he was talking about and I am afraid most of the others attending the meeting were in similar straits. It took me another thirty years of interaction before I began to appreciate fully what McCulloch had to say, and one of my fondest memories is the week McCulloch spent with us at Stanford discussing his insights and ours just before his death.

Exciting as all of these Chicago experiences were, they did not furnish me with some of the basic tools I needed to accomplish my basic goals, which were: To explore the relationship between brain function and mental processes such as emotion, cognition, and conation. In my search for a hay fever-free location where I might earn my living as a neurosurgeon and at the same time pursue these goals, I heard of the Yerkes Laboratories of Primate Biology near Jacksonville Florida. Fortunately, there was a position open in Jacksonville with J. G. Lyerly, who had devised an improved (superior) approach to frontal lobotomy that was safer than the classical Freeman-Watts procedure and left fewer unwanted side effects. I took my Florida State Board Examinations and began practice.

Lyerly agreed that I might work two half-days per week, plus any free time, for my research at Yerkes. I called Lashley and he responded favorably, stating that he had been looking for a neurosurgeon to assist him in his primate neuropsychological research. Thus began a collaboration which was to prove most influential in shaping the subsequent research program.

Lashley taught me the techniques of experimental psychology, a field of inquiry that I did not know existed. True I had watched Ward Halstead at work in Chicago but had been unimpressed. Nothing that Halstead had done led to any insights into how the brain functioned. Paradoxically, although Lashley was almost solopsistic in his approach and interpretations, he provided many of the insights that led to the discoveries which make up the substance of this report. The discoveries we made while he was still alive, such as the unique relationship of the frontolimbic forebrain to delayed alternation behavior and the sensory specificity of various sectors of the posterior "association" cortex, he tried to ignore. But always, his critical wit sharpened our interpretations and provided the basis for further observation and experiment.

The opportunity to work full time in research and thus make these observations and experiments came when I was asked by John Fulton to join him in the Department of Physiology at Yale University. My association with Yale lasted for a decade, during which time I also directed the research laboratories of the Institute of Living, a mental hospital in nearby Hartford, Connecticut. The facilities at Yale and in Hartford provided ample space for a group of young investigators dedicated to exploring the power of combining the techniques of experimental psychology with those of neurophysiology and experimental neurosurgery. Doctoral students from Yale (e.g., Martha Helson Wilson); Harvard (e.g., Lawrence Weiskrance); McGill (e.g., Mortimer Mishkin); University of California at Berkeley (e.g., William Wilson); and Stanford (e.g., Jerome Schwartzbaum) formed a nucleus of a most productive team, all of whom received their degrees while working on the program.

During this period I spent a month a year at the Yerkes Laboratory, and Kao Liang Chow, an early collaborator, spent a month with me in the north, reestablishing at least in part Yerkes' original vision for his primate research laboratories. This continuing collaboration led to an invitation to succeed Lashley as director of the laboratories, and I filled this post until the president of Yale University sold the laboratories to Emory University in Atlanta.

Also during this period, I began an intimate association with psychologists at Harvard University. I taught summer school there one year; built operant equipment in the Harvard shops and learned a great deal from S. S. Stevens, Gary Boring, and Georg von Bekesy. Once a month, Bert Rosner and I drove up to Harvard (and later MIT) to perform experiments with Walter Rosenblith on monkeys in which we evoked electrical potentials in the cortex by auditory stimulation. Somewhat later, these sessions were extended to explore, with Wolfgang Kohler, the evocation of DC (direct current) shifts under similar conditions.

My interactions with B. F. Skinner were especially memorable and led to a decade of primate operant conditioning experiments which developed into subsequent research in cognitive neuropsychology. Ultimately, I was able to automate the operant equipment by designing a computer-controlled panel dubbed: "Discrimination Apparatus for Discrete Trial Analysis" (DADTA).

At one point in our interaction, Skinner and I came to an impasse over the possible mechanism involved in the chaining of responses. Chaining was disrupted by resections of the far frontal cortex. Skinner suggested that proprioceptive feedback might have been disrupted, but this hypothesis was not supported by my experiments. Furthermore, as I indicated to Skinner, he as a biologist could propose such an hypothesis, but I, as a loyal Skinnerian, had to search elsewhere than the "black box" for an answer to our question. George Miller overheard some of our discussions and pointed out to us that he had available an apparatus that made chaining of responses easy: a computer. Miller explained to me the principles of list programming that he had just learned form Herbert Simon and Alan Newell. The culmination of the collaboration begun by that chance encounter in the halls of Harvard was *Plans and the Structure of*

Behavior, a book influenced also by interactions with Jerome Bruner. The book was written in 1960 at the Center for Advanced Studies in the Behavioral Sciences, adjacent to the campus of Stanford University.

Thanks to Jack Hilgard and Robert Sears of the Psychology Department, and to Tom Gonda in Psychiatry, I was given an appointment at Stanford. During the twenty-five years since my departure from Yale and Harvard, the research therefore has been carried out at Stanford University aided by a lifetime research career award from the United States Department of Health and Human Services.

At Stanford another group of associates, both doctoral and postdoctoral, joined the program. (Altogether, some 50 theses have been completed under its aegis.) Daniel Kimble, Robert Douglas, James Dewson, Muriel Bagshaw, and Leslie Ungerleider were among those who made major contributions. And Nico Spinelli became an integral and almost indispensible collaborator. The results of these, the previous, and subsequent research collaborations can be organized into overlapping phases, each phase representing a problem area and the application of techniques appropriate to that problem area.

Research Phases

Phase I.   At the time my research program began, large areas of the primate cortex remained silent to experimental investigation. In humans, damage to these areas resulted in agnosias and aphasia, and in changes in interpersonal emotional interactions. But it was not known whether these changes in competence and behavior were the result of damage to primary sensory-motor system, or whether the changes could occur without such damage. Furthermore, it was not known whether the changes were specific to one or another location within the silent cortex.

By using a battery of behavioral tests and resecting large extents of the silent cortex of monkeys without invading the primary sensory-motor systems, answers to these questions were achieved relatively rapidly. A method was devised that compared (using superimpositions of reconstructions) by summing across the extent of the resections that produced a particular behavioral deficit, and subtracting the sum of the extent of the resections that produced no deficit. This "intercept of sums" technique allowed us to make multiple dissociations among the various deficits produced by the resections and to localize the brain system involved in the behavior represented by each task.

The results were unequivocal. One type of deficit was produced when the far frontal, medial, and basal cortex were resected. Another type of deficit followed resections of the posterior cortical convexity and this type could be further subdivided into sensory specific components, each of which was related to its own portion of the convexal cortex. In no instance was invasion of the adjacent primary sensory-motor systems critical to producing the deficit or even in enhancing it.

Phase II.   Having established various specific behavioral indicators for the functions of these areas of the cortex, the next problem was to discover the psychological meaning of the indicators. Much as a Babinsky sign is an indicator of improper functioning of the spinal pyramidal motor system, we now had available signs of malfunction of brain cognitive and related systems.

In order to define the meaning of the behavioral indicators we had to explore the limiting factors for these deficits in a wide range of behavioral tasks. Some of these limits could be established by factorial designs that we used to explore the visual deficit produced by resections of the inferotemporal cortex. Discriminations of color, brightness, size, two- and three-dimensional shapes proved sensitive to the cortical resection. At other times parametric designs had to be invoked, as when we wanted to know the limits of the brightness or size discrimination deficits. But even these experimental procedures often failed to provide sufficiently precise answers. Response operator characteristic curves (ROC) were explored in order to check whether the deficiency produced was a function of changes in detection threshold or in response bias.

The results of this phase of the program yielded a wealth of data. However interpretation was seldom straightforward, in part due to the lack of agreement about the constructs used in experimental psychology. Just how does one compare the results obtained in a fixed interval operant conditioning study with a result obtained in an ROC decisional experiment? How does one compare either of these with results obtained in a delayed alternation situation tested in a Yerkes box or the DADTA machine? Interpretations have been made after much crossvalidation of techniques, often using the same subjects and, of course, comparable resections. But in most cases some conceptual leaps were necessary in making the interpretations and these leaps were guided by findings on human neuropsychological patients.

Phase III.   Another line of research, made possible by the initial findings of Phase I, was an attempt at specification of the anatomy and physiological mechanisms of operation of the neural systems of which the critical cortical areas were a part. Chemical and electrical stimulations in anesthetized or problem-solving monkeys were performed. And the effects of such stimulations on electrical recordings of event related potentials (ERP) were assessed while monkeys performed in the DADTA. Also, such effects on the microstructure of receptive fields of single units in the visual system were assayed.

Once again the results of these experiments yielded a good deal of data which are interesting in their own right. However, as in Phase II, interpretation and in some instances controversial interpretation became necessary. One major controversy centers on whether the sensory specificity of the convexal "association" cortex is due to its transcortical *input* via connections from the related primary sensory cortex, or whether the specificity is to be ascribed to an *output* which operates down-stream on the primary sensory systems. We were able to make massive disconnections, some of which appear to be complete, between the primary sensory systems (at both the thalamic and cortical levels) and the inferotemporal cortex involved in visual discriminations. None of these disconnections produced lasting deficits in sensory discriminations and this led me to propose the output hypothesis. The controversy hinges solely on whether the disconnections are in fact total, as it is suggested by input theorists that even a small remnant of connectivity is believed sufficient to mediate an input.

Phase IV.   The research program began with the aim to clarify the brain mechanisms involved in cognitive, conative, and emotional processes in humans. The final research phase of the program therefore must address the relevance of the results of the non-human primate research, in which some 1500 monkeys were used, to human neuropsychological findings. Since my early days in the neurosurgical clinic, electrical recordings of event related scalp potentials, computerized tomography, and nuclear magnetic resonance tech-

niques have been developed to aid in the localization of brain patho-
logical conditions. The battery of tests developed by experimental
psychologists is also a recent innovation. Several members of the
neuropsychological laboratories at Stanford are currently using these
tools to provide a basis for comparison of non-human and human
neuropsychological data.

Phase V. The laboratory research has yielded many unexpected
results. These results have dramatically changed my views from time
to time and posed, as critical to further research, problems that I had
thought I could ignore. Much of my theoretical work has stemmed
from these surprises.

Discoveries

Karl Popper has claimed that science is based on conjecture and
refutation, and Karl Lashley was always most comfortable when he
operated in this mode. My own research appears to have proceeded in
a somewhat more haphazard fashion. Despite the planning represented in the phases described above, the actual research was more
truly a search that stemmed from problems and paradoxes (such as
unexpectedly finding relatively direct sensory inputs to the motor
cortex) rather than from well formulated conjectures or hypotheses.

Theses there were, but only rarely did I derive single testable
hypo-theses with experiments designed to confirm or disconfirm.
Rather, the rule was that several more or less clearly defined alternatives presented themselves once the thesis, the reason(s) for performing the research, became clear. Experiments were designed to find
out which of the alternatives fit the data obtained. Sometimes the data
fit none of the alternatives, the thesis itself was found wanting, and
new directions had to be taken. Often these new directions stemmed
from attempts to systematize the data already obtained and to develop
an appropriate frame for sorting and classifying them.

Whatever the merits or deficiencies of this approach, it is shared by
many biologists. Claude Bernard, when asked how he proceeded in
the laboratory, answered that he simply asked nature some questions.
By adopting this perspective, the yield in my program has been
substantial and many discoveries were made which may not have
been uncovered by a more rigid methodological approach. Some of
these are detailed below:

1.   Delineation of a mediobasal motor cortex defined the bound-
aries of the limbic forebrain and established the relationship between
limbic cortex and visceroautonomic activity. Based on the earlier
work of McCulloch, Bailey, and von Bonin, we established by
strychnine neuronography and by electrical stimulation and histo-
logical examination, the interrelationship between the amygdaloid
complex and the surrounding orbitofrontal, anterior insular, and
temporal polar cortex and the relationship of all of these to the limbic
forebrain.

The work of Arthur Ward and Robert Livingston had established
that visceroautonomic responses were obtained from electrical stimulation of the cingulate gyrus and orbitofrontal cortex. We extended
these results to the anterior insula, temporal pole, and amygdala.

Thus the entire anterior portion of the limbic forebrain was shown
to constitute a mediobasal motor cortex that regulates peripheral
visceroautonomic functions.

2.   Establishing the fact that the far frontal cortex is the "association" cortex for the limbic forebrain accounted for the psychosurgi-
cal effects of frontal lobotomy. Using the delayed response and
delayed alternation techniques we extended the work of Carlysle
Jacobsen and Henry Nissen, who had shown that resections of far
frontal cortex disrupted performance on these tasks. We found that
resections of the various structures composing the limbic forebrain
(hippocampus, amygdala, cingulate cortex) and lesions of the head of
the caudate nucleus also disrupted performance of delayed alternation (but not of delayed response). We also found that resections of
the cortex of the posterior cerebral convexity failed to disrupt performance on these tasks; if anything, monkeys with such resections
tended to perform better than their unoperated control subjects.

These findings, and anatomical considerations involving the organization of the projections from the dorsal thalamus to the cortex,
indicated that the far frontal cortex can be considered the "association" or higher processing cortex for the limbic forebrain. This
relationship between the far frontal cortex and the limbic forebrain
helped account to some extent for the changes produced by frontal
lobotomy in humans.

3.   Controls on visceroautonomic activities by the frontolimbic
forebrain were shown to serve as boosters for habituation and conditioning. A great deal of effort went into a determination of the
functions of the frontolimbic forebrain. As noted, the anterior por-

tions of this cortex proved to constitute a visceroautonomic motor cortex. The nature of the control over visceroautonomic functions by the amygdala, the "funnel" or critical focus of this motor system, was demonstrated in a series of experiments on habituation of the orienting reaction and of conditioning in fully awake monkeys.

The results of these experiments showed that the visceroautonomic components (galvanic skin conductance, heart and respiratory rates, and adrenocortical responses) of orienting (and conditioning) failed to occur in amydgalectomized monkeys who also failed to habituate the behavioral components of orienting. I concluded that the visceroautonomic components of orienting acted as a "booster" to help register novel events. Without such a booster, familiarization, habituation, could not occur. Similar results were obtained by James McGaugh in his long series of studies on the consolidation of the memory trace.

The experiments using the orienting reaction were extended to monkeys and patients with far frontal lesions with results essentially the same as those obtained with amygdalectomized subjects.

4.   The frontolimbic regulation of visceroautonomic activity was shown not to be devoid of sensory guidance: The intensive (protocritic) aspects of pain and temperature sensory inputs were demonstrated to reach the frontolimbic, not the parietal, cortex. The possible sensory input to the frontolimbic forebrain was not ignored. Pain threshold was shown unaffected, but avoidance conditioning was disrupted by all resections which invaded the far frontal or limbic formations including amygdala, hippocampus, and cingulate cortex.

Taste (using bitters) threshold discrimination was shown to be disrupted by resections of the anterior portion of the planum temporalis just forward of the primary auditory input area (and no other cortical resection). And after resections of the temporal pole, monkeys would repeatedly eat meat (hot dogs), something which control monkeys do not do. Thus the anterior portion of the planum temporalis serves as the primary receiving cortex for taste while the temporal polar cortex serves a higher level of gustatory processing.

Temperature discrimination was disrupted by electrical resections and electrical stimulations in the region of the orbitofrontal and anterior insular cortex and the amygdala. No such disruption was seen after resections or electrical stimulations of parietal cortex.

I summarized these findings with a proposal, derived from a distinction made by Henry Head, that the frontolimbic forebrain processes the "protocritic" aspects of sensation while the systems of the cortical convexity process the "epicritic" aspects. Epicritic sensations display local sign (i.e., can be accurately localized in time and space). The protocritic aspects of sensation are devoid of local sign and may reflect the bandwidth of tolerances for an *intensive* dimension of sensations.

5.   The sensory-specific aspects of cognitive processes were shown to be dependent on the sensory specificity of restricted regions within the posterior "association" cortex of the cortical convexity: With the exception of taste (and the vestibular sense), the various end stations of the epicritic aspects of sensation in the cortex of the cerebral convexity were well known when this program of research was initiated. At that time it was thought that the expanse of cortex lying between the primary sensory receiving areas served as "associative" function. As noted, the sensory specificity of agnosias found in human patients was thought to result from lesions of the association cortex which invaded the adjacent primary sensory cortex as well.

The multiple dissociation technique demonstrated that, in the monkey, no such invasion of primary sensory cortex was necessary to produce the sensory specific deficits which occur after resections of the "association" cortex. An area specific to the tactile sense, another to hearing, and a third, specific to vision, were located.

A long series of experiments centered on the functions of the inferotemporal cortex, the area shown to be specific to vision. The results of this series showed that, while visual sensory functions such as threshold and detection remained essentially intact, resections produced marked deficits whenever selections among visual imputs were demanded.

Electrical recordings of event related potentials gave similar results. Recordings made from the primary visual cortex were sensitive to changes in numbers and kinds of features which characterized the input. Recordings made from the inferotemporal cortex were sensitive to variables which influenced selection or "choice," especially when this was difficult.

Selection was interpreted to be a cognitive, information process which, when disturbed by a brain lesion in humans, results in an agnosia.

6.   Preliminary evidence was provided to show that perceptual constancy is a function of the perisensory systems: Selection among alternatives implies that these alternatives are clearly categorized. Categorizing, in turn, implies object constancy. In one experiment

we showed that object constancy was not related to the functions of
the frontolimbic forebrain. In another study, size constancy was
disrupted by a combined lesion of the pulvinar of the thalamus and the
peristriate cortex from which eye movements are obtained by electrical stimulation. Following such lesions monkeys responded to the
size of the retinal image and did not take distance cues into account.

Although these are only first steps, the results of these experiments
suggest that object constancy will be found to be a function of the
systems of the posterior cerebral convexity, most likely of the perisensory thalamocortical systems, and that the functions of these
perisensory systems devolve on their control of motor mechanisms.

7.   Reciprocity was demonstrated between the functions of the
frontolimbic systems and those of the cortical convexity: A Jackso-
nian reciprocity was demonstrated to exist between the functions of
the frontolimbic formations and those of the cortex of cortical convexity. Resections of the frontolimbic cortex actually speeded learning of sensory discriminations while making the learning of delayed
alternation well nigh impossible. Resections of the cortex of the
posterior convexity actually speeded learning of delayed alternation
while making the learning of difficult sensory discriminations well
nigh impossible.

This reciprocity was also demonstrated with electrophysiological
techniques. Recovery cycles in the visual system were shortened by
electrical stimulations of structures within the frontolimbic forebrain. Receptive fields of neurons in the lateral geniculate nucleus
and in the primary visual cortex were made smaller by electrical
stimulations of the systems of the posterior convexity and made
larger by stimulations of frontolimbic systems.

8.   It was shown that actions, defined as the consequences of
behavior (in addition to muscles and movements), are represented in
the precentral motor cortex. The reciprocity of effects of resections
and stimulations of frontolimbic and posterior convexal systems on
the functions of the primary sensory receiving areas and the involvement of motor control in the production of object constancy, inspired
us to look more closely at some aspects of the functions of the primary
motor and sensory systems.

As noted, quite by accident we discovered direct cutaneous and
proprioceptive inputs to the precentral motor cortex. We also explored the effects on behavior of extensive resections of this cortex
using latch boxes and cinematographic recordings of the behavior of
monkeys in a variety of situations. The results of these investigations

showed (as had the clinical evidence noted earlier) that all movements remained intact, but that skills in certain learned situations (latch boxes) were impaired: Though the sequencing of behavior was not disrupted, transition time between behavioral elements increased markedly.

I concluded that the precentral cortex exerted control over behavioral "acts" (defined as the consequences of movements) rather than control over specific movements or muscles. Control over acts involved control over movements and muscles, of course, but the nature of the higher level control had in some way to encode the *consequences* of movements rather than specific muscle sequences per se.

9.   The possibility that this representation devolved on a spectral analysis of changing loads was tested and neurons in the sensory-motor cortex were shown to be selective of bandwidths of the frequency of a movement. The nature of the encoding process remained opaque to me for almost a decade after completing the initial experiments. Then, a series of events occurred which allowed us to continue the explorations. First, data obtained by Ed Evarts showed that the activity of neurons in the precentral motor cortex was proportional to the load placed on a lever manipulated by a monkey and not, per se, the extension or tension of the muscles used in the manipulation. Second, the results obtained by N. Bernstein in the Soviet Union were translated into English. Bernstein had shown that he could predict the course of a more or less repetitive series of actions by performing a Fourier analysis of the wave forms produced by spots placed over the joints involved in the action.

By this time I had developed the thesis that certain aspects of cortical function could best be understood in terms of orthogonal (linear) transforms of sensory inputs, such as the Fourier. We therefore performed an experiment in which we examined whether neurons in the cat motor cortex were turned to certain bandwidths of frequencies of passive movements of their forelimbs. Here we were testing a specific hypothesis, and the hypothesis was confirmed.

My interpretation of these results is that the motor cortex computes, in the transform domain, a set of values which, when inversely transformed, represent the consequences to be achieved by an act (e.g., load to be lifted).

10.   Single neurons in the visual cortex select were shown to select a variety of input features and they were shown to differ in the conjunction of selectivities which characterized them. Thus the

common assumption that single neurons serve as feature detectors or channels needs further exploration. Explorations of unit activity in the primary visual system were based on the work of Kuffler, Hubel and Wiesel, and the many other investigators who took up such investigations. Our concern was to try to classify the many properties of visual receptive fields. For several years we attempted to make a classification of cells (as is the common procedure). But we found that each cortical cell had conjoined selectivity to several feature properties and that different cells displayed different conjunctions. We are currently investigating whether the output of a cell is specific to a specific feature, or whether the cell simply responds that it has been stimulated. If the cell simply responds, then feature encoding would be a function of a spatial configuration of an *ensemble* of neurons and not a particular cell.

Theory

1.   The publication of *Plans and the Structure of Behavior* had a major impact on moving psychology from a strictly behavioristic stimulus-response or response-reward stance to a more cognitive approach. In that publication, George Miller, Eugene Galanter, and I called ourselves "subjective behaviorists." I have already noted how I became involved with Miller after reaching an impasse on the problem of the chaining of responses. Clinical considerations, set forth in my contribution to Sigmund Koch's *Psychology as a Science,* were also instrumental in taking more seriously the verbal reports of introspection than was the custom in midcentury. Thus came about the major divergence from Skinner, who abhors the use of subjective terminology.

The thrust of *Plans* was that computers and computer programs can serve as powerful metaphors for understanding cognitive processes and the brain mechanisms involved in them. That thrust has been realized to some extent in the neuroscience community as well as in psychology in that many aspects of complex behavioral functioning are now conceptualized in terms of "information processing," and the initiation of "motor programs."

However, it has also become clear that brain mechanisms are considerably different, even in the fundamentals of their operation, from current serial processing computers. Brain mechanisms rely to a large extent on parallel processing, which suggests that addressing occurs by content rather than by location. Our mails are representative of location addressable systems. Content addressable systems are akin to those in which a broadcast is receivable by a properly tuned instrument, irrespective of location within the broadcast region.

2.   These differences were highlighted in *Languages of the Brain*, published a decade after *Plans*. *Languages* continued to explore the power of hierarchically arranged information processing mechanisms but added the mechanisms of image processing which, though they had been integral to the conceptions proposed in *Plans*, were not explored because no appropriate metaphor was available at that time. Image construction depends on parallel processing and thus is better fitted to some aspects of brain anatomy and function than is serial programming.

One of the consequences of considering parallel as well as serial processing was the introduction of a model for feedforward operations. In *Plans* we had made much of hierarchically organized feedback loops. As Roger Brown pointed out in his review of the volume, this left the mental apparatus almost as much at the mercy of input as did the earlier stimulus-response psychologies. In *Languages* this deficiency was remedied by showing that coactivation of two or more feedback loops by a parallel input would produce the kind of feedforward organization basic to voluntary control. This proposal was in consonance with similar suggestions put forward by Helmholtz, Ross Ashby, Roger Sperry, and Hans-Lukas Teuber, but was more specific in its design features than were the earlier suggestions.

3.   Of the many languages described in *Languages of the Brain*, the language of the hologram has had the greatest impact—as noted in the introduction. This impact is due to the fact that the optical hologram displays vividly the operations of image processing. Image processing relies on orthogonal transformations such as the Fourier, which because of their linearity are readily invertible. This means that image and transform are reciprocals, i.e., duals of one another and that transformation in either direction is readily achieved.

The transform domain has properties that make it ideal for storage and for computation. Millions of decabits of retrievable information can be encoded in a centimeter cube of holographic memory. IBM uses such storage devices in the machines that read the stripes which identify grocery store items. Correlations are computed by simple convolving (multiplying) one input with the next. This accounts for the value of the fast Fourier transform (FFT) in statistics.

There are other properties of the transform domain which are not so obviously useful but which have had a tremendous theoretical impact. Information becomes distributed in the transform domain so that essentially equivalent images can be reconstructed from any portion of the stored representation. Again, radio or television broadcasting makes a good analogy. At any location within the reach of the broadcast, the coded representations of all of the programs are intermingled. Nonetheless, each program is available through an inverse transformation of the code by an appropriate tuning device. The whole spectrum is enfolded into every portion of space and each part represents the whole: Thus the name, hologram.

Holography was a mathematical invention designed by Dennis Gabor to enhance the resolution of electron microscopy. Optical realizations of the mathematics came only a decade later, and it is necessary to emphasize that other realizations of the mathematics such as those made by computer (as in the IBM example above) are equally valid. To the extent that certain aspects of brain function realize Gabor's mathematics, to that extent they can be thought of as holographic. As there is considerable evidence that one of the properties of receptive fields of cells in the primary visual cortex can be expressed in terms of Gabor functions, there is some merit to pursuing a holographic hypothesis of brain processes with regard to perception and memory.

The enfolding process which characterizes the transform domain provides additional properties which have seized the imagination of scientists and the public. The dimensions which characterize the transform domain are very different from the familiar space-time dimensions which characterize the image domain. Consider for instance the dimensions of a spectral representation of an electroencephalographic record: Its dimensions are frequency and power. Time has been enfolded into the frequency domain.

Causality is a casualty in a domain that enfolds space-time. Thus, ordinary Newtonian-Cartesian-Euclidian mechanics no longer hold until the inverse transformation into the image domain is realized. My interpretation of these attributes of transformation is that the transform domain characterizes potential rather than actual realizations.

The implications of this interpretation are detailed elsewhere. I would not be surprised to read some version in OMNI one of these days. For now, I will finish by noting what a fantastic adventure it has been to explore our world within—an adventure equal to that experienced in expeditions of yore to polar and equatorial territories. And I look forward to continuing emergence of new vistas in the brain and behavioral sciences at this fascinating frontier.

DATA PAPERS

I. Brain Systems Analysis: The selective effect on behavior of brain stimulations and resections.

A. Resections

D-4. Blum, J. S., Chow, K. L., & Pribram, K. H. A behavioral analysis of the organization of the parieto-temporo-preoccipital cortex. *J. Comp. Neurol.*, 1950, *93*, pp. 53–100.

D-10. Pribram, K. H., Mishkin, M., Rosvold, H. E., & Kaplan, S. J. Effects on delayed-response performance of lesions of dorso-lateral and ventromedial frontal cortex of baboons. *J. Comp. Physiol. Psychol.*, 1952, *45*, pp. 565–575.

D-11. Pribram, K. H., Chow, K. L., & Semmes, J. Limit and organization of the cortical projection from the medial thalamic nucleus in monkeys. *J. Comp. Neurol.*, 1953, *95*, pp. 433–440.

D-12. Pribram, K. H. & Bagshaw, M. Further analysis of the temporal lobe syndrome utilizing fronto-temporal ablations. *J. Comp. Neurol.*, 1953, *99*, pp. 347–375.

D-17. Bagshaw, M. H. & Pribram, K. H. Cortical organization in gustation (Macaca Mulatta). *J. Neurophysiol.*, 1953, *16*, pp. 399–508.

D-20. Mishkin, M. & Pribram, K. H. Visual discrimination performance following partial ablations of the temporal lobe. I. Ventral vs. lateral. *J. Comp. Physiol. Psychol.*, 1954, *47*, pp. 14–20.

D-22. Pribram, K. H. Concerning three rhinencephalic systems. *Electroenceph. Clin. Neurophysiol.*, 1954, *6*, pp. 708–709.

D-25. Pribram, K. H. Lesions of "frontal eye fields" and delayed response of baboons. *J. Neurophysiol.*, 1955, *18*, pp. 105–112.

D-27. Chow, K. L. & Pribram, K. H. Cortical projection of the thalamic ventrolateral nuclear group in monkeys. *J. Comp. Neurol.*, 1956, *104*, pp. 37–75.

D-30. Pribram, K. H. & Bary, J. Further behavioral analysis of the parieto-temporo-preoccipital cortex. *J. Neurophysiol.*, 1956, *19*, pp. 99–106.

D-32. Pribram, K. H. & Weiskrantz, L. A comparison of the effects of medial and lateral cerebral resections on conditioned avoidance behavior in monkeys. *J. Comp. Physiol. Psychol.*, 1957, *50*, pp. 74–80.

D-34. Pribram, K. H. On the neurology of thinking. *Behav. Sci.*, 1959, *4*, pp. 265–287.

D-71. Dewson, J. H., III, Pribram, K. H. & Lynch, J. Effects of abalations of temporal cortex on speech sound discrimination in monkeys. *Exp. Neurol.*, 1969, *24*, pp. 579–591.

D-96. Christensen, C. A. & Pribram, K. H. The visual discrimination performance of monkeys with foveal prestriate and inferotemporal lesions. *Physiol. & Behav.*, 1977, *18*, pp. 403–407.

D-98. Brody, B. A., Ungerleider, L. G. & Pribram, K. H. The effects of instability of the visual display on pattern discrimination learning by monkeys: Dissociation produced after resections of frontal and inferotemporal cortex. *Neuropsychologia*, 1977, *15*, pp. 439–448.

B. Electrical and chemical stimulations and epileptogenic foci

D-1. Bucy, P. C. & Pribram, K. H. Localized sweating as part of a localized convulsive seizure. *Arch. Neurol. & Psychiat.*, 1943, *50*, pp. 456–461.

D-2. Kaada, B. R., Pribram, K. H., & Epstein, J. A. Respiratory and vascular responses in monkeys from temporal pole, insula, orbital surface and congulate gyrus. *J. Neurophysiol*, 1949, *12*, pp. 347–356.

D-3. Fulton, J. F., Pribram, K. H., Stevenson, J. A. F., & Wall, P. Interrelations between orbital gyrus, insula, temporal tip and anterior cingulate gyrus. *Trans. Am. Neurol. Assoc.*, 1949, pp. 175–179.

D-5. Pribram, K. H., Lennox, M. A., & Dunsmore, R. H. Some connections of the orbito-fronto-temporal limbic and hippocampal areas of Macaca Mulatta. *J. Neurophysiol*, 1950, *13*, pp. 127–135.

D-7. Lennox, M. A., Dunsmore, R. H., Epstein, K. A., & Pribram, K. H. Electrocorticographic effects of stimulation of posterior orbital, temporal and cingulate areas of Macaca Mulatta. *J. Neurophysiol.*, 1950, *13*, pp. 383–388.

D-8. Wall, P. D. & Pribram, K. H. Trigeminal neurotomy and blood pressure responses from stimulation of lateral central cortex of Macaca Mulatta. *J. Neurophysiol.*, 1950, *13*, pp. 409–412.

D-9. Pribram, K. H. Some aspects of experimental psychosurgery: The effect of scarring frontal cortex on complex behavior. *Surgical Forum*, 1951, *36*, pp. 315–318.

D-14. Malis, L. I., Pribram, K. H., & Kruger, L. Action potentials in "motor" cortex evoked by peripheral nerve stimulation. *J. Neurophysiol.*, 1953, *16*, pp. 161–167.

D-15. Maclean, P. D. & Pribram, K. H. Neuronographic analysis of medial and basal cerebral cortex. I. Cat. *J. Neurophysiol.*, 1953, *16*, pp. 312–323.

D-16. Pribram, K. H. & Maclean, P. D. Neuronographic analysis of medial and basal cerebral cortex. II. Monkey. *J. Neurophysiol.*, 1953, *16*, pp. 324–340.

D-18. Pribram, K. H., Rosner, B. S., & Rosenblith, W. A. Electrical responses to acoustic clicks in monkeys: Extent of neocortex activated. *J. Neurophysiol.*, 1954, *17*, pp. 366–384.

D-35. Kraft, M., Obrist, W. D., & Pribram, K. H. The effect of irritative lesions of the striate cortex on learning of visual discrimination in monkeys. *J. Comp. Physiol. Psychol.*, 1960, *53*, pp. 17–22.

D-36. Stamm, J. S. & Pribram, K. H. Effects of epileptogenic lesions on frontal cortex on learning and retention in monkeys. *J. Neurophysiol.*, 1960, *23*, pp. 552–563.

D-40. Stamm, J. S. & Pribram, K. H. Effects of epileptogenic lesions in infero-temporal cortex on learning and retention in monkeys. *J. Comp. Physiol. Psychol.*, 1961, *54*, pp. 614–618.

D-61. Pribram, K. H., Blehert, S. R. & Spinelli, D. N. Effects on visual discrimination of crosshatching and undercutting the inferotemporal cortex of monkeys. *J. Comp. Physiol. Psychol.*, 1966, *62*, pp. 358–364.

D-68. Pribram, K. H., Spinelli, D. N. & Reitz, S. L. The effects of radical disconnection of occipital and temporal cortex on visual behaviour of monkeys. *Brain*, 1969, *92*, pp. 301–312.

D-74. Reitz, S. L. & Pribram, K. H. Some subcortical connections of the inferotemporal gyrus of monkey. *Exp. Neurol.*, 1969, *25*, pp. 632–645.

NLP-38. Reitz, S. L. & Gerbrandt, L. K. Pre- and post-trial temporal lobe seizures in monkeys and memory consolidation. *J. Comp. Physiol. Psychol.*, 1971, *74*, pp. 179–184.

II. Experimental Analysis of Behaviors Related to Brain Systems

A. Limbic

D-19. Pribram, K. H. & Fulton, J. F. An experimental critique of the effects of anterior cingulate ablations in monkey. *Brain*, 1954, *77*, pp. 34–44.

D-21.   Rosvold, H. E., Mirsky, A. J., & Pribram, K. H. Influence of amygdalectomy on social behavior in monkeys. *J. Comp. Physiol. Psychol.*, 1954, *47*, pp. 173–178.

D-31.   Fuller, J. L., Rosvold, H. E., & Pribram, K. H. The effect on affective and cognitive behavior in the dog of lesions of the pyriform-amygdala-hippocampal complex. *J. Comp. Physiol. Psychol.*, 1957, *50*, pp. 89–96.

D-33.   Mirsky, A. J., Rosvold, H. E., & Pribram, K. H. Effects of cingulectomy on social behavior in monkeys. *J. Neurophysiol.*, 1957, *20*, pp. 588–601.

D-37.   Schwartzbaum, J. S. & Pribram, K. H. The effects of amygdalectomy in monkeys on transposition along a brightness continuum. *J. Comp. Physiol. Psychol.*, 1960, *53*, pp. 396–399.

D-41.   Pribram, K. H., Wilson, W. A. & Connors, J. The effects of lesions of the medial forebrain on alternation behavior of rhesus monkeys. *Exp. Neurol.*, 1962, *6*, pp. 36–47.

D-45.   Kimble, D. P. & Pribram, K. H. Hippocampectomy and behavior sequences. *Science*, 1963, *139*, pp. 824–825.

D-47.   Hearst, E. & Pribram, K. H. Facilitation of avoidance behavior in unavoidable shocks in normal and amygdalectomized monkeys. *Psych. Reports*, 1964, *14*, pp. 39–42.

D-48.   Hearst, E. & Pribram, K. H. Appetitive and aversive generalization gradients in normal and amygdalectomized monkeys. *J. Comp. Physiol. Psychol.*, 1964, *58*, pp. 296–298.

D-50.   Bagshaw, M. H. & Pribram, K. H. Effect of amygdalectomy on transfer of training in monkeys. *J. Comp. Physiol. Psychol.*, 1965, *59*, pp. 118–121.

D-56.   Douglas, R. J. & Pribram, K. H. Learning and limbic lesions. *Neuropsychologia*, 1966, *4*, pp. 197–220.

D-57.   Pribram, K. H., Lim, H., Poppen, R., & Bagshaw, M. H. Limbic lesions and the temporal structure of redundancy. *J. Comp. Physiol. Psychol.*, 1966, *61*, pp. 365–373.

D-69.   Douglas, R. J., Barrett, T. W., Pribram, K. H. & Cerny, M. C. Limbic lesions and error reduction. *J. Comp. Physiol. Psychol.*, 1969, *68*, pp. 437–441.

D-70.   Douglas, R. J. & Pribram, K. H. Distraction and habituation in monkeys with limbic lesions. *J. Comp. Physiol. Psychol.*, 1969, *69*, pp. 473–480.

D-72.   Pribram, K. H., Douglas, R. & Pribram, B. J. The nature of non-limbic learning. *J. Comp. Physiol. Psychol.*, 1969, *69*, pp. 765–772.

D-87.   Spevak, A. A. & Pribram, K. H. A decisional analysis of the effects of limbic lesions on learning in monkeys *J. Comp. Physiol. Psychol.*, 1973, *82*, pp. 211–226.

D-91.   Chin, J., Pribram, K. H., Drake, K. H. & Greene, J. Disruption of temperature discrimination during limbic forebrain stimulation in monkeys. *Neuropsychologia*, 1976, *14*, pp. 293–310.

D-102.   Pribram, K. H., Reitz, S., McNeil, M. & Spevack, A. A. The effect of amygdalectomy on orienting and classical conditioning. *Pavlovian J. Biol. Sci.*, 1979, *14*, pp. 203–217.

NLP-5.   Douglas, R. J. Transposition, novelty, and limbic lesions. *J. Comp. Physiol. Psychol.*, 1966, *62*, pp. 354–357.

NLP-25. Barrett, T. W. Studies of the function of the amygdaloid complex in Macaca Mulatta. *Neuropsychologia*, 1969, *7*, pp. 1–12.

NLP-26. Barrett, T. W. A theoretical analysis of the effects of amygdalectomy and of organismic motivation. *Math. Biosci.*, 1969, *4*, pp. 153–178.

B. Frontal

D-6.   Pribram, K. H. Some physical and pharmacological factors affecting delayed response performance of baboons following frontal lobotomy. *J. Neurophysiol, 1950, 13*, pp. 373–382.

D-13.   Mishkin, M., Rosvold, H. E., & Pribram, K. H. Effects of nembutol in baboons with frontal lesions. *J. Neurophysiol.*, 1953, *14*, pp. 155–159.

D-24.   Mishkin, M. & Pribram, K. H. Analysis of the effects of frontal lesions in monkey: I. Variations of delayed alternation. *J. Comp. Physiol. Psychol.*, 1955, *48*, pp. 492–495.

D-28.   Miskin, M. & Pribram, K. H. Analysis of the effects of frontal lesions in monkey: II. Variation of delayed response. *J. Comp. Physiol. Psychol.*, 1956, *49*, pp. 36–40.

D-29.   Pribram, K. H. & Miskin, M. Analysis of the effects of frontal lesions in monkey: III. Object alternation. *J. Comp. Physiol. Psychol.*, 1956, *49*, pp. 41–45.

D-39.   Pribram, K. H. A further experimental analysis of the behavioral deficit that follows injury to the primate frontal cortex. *Exp. Neurol.*, 1961, *3*, pp. 432–466.

D-46.   Luria, A. R., Pribram, K. H. & Homskaya, E. D. An experimental analysis of the behavioral disturbance produced by a left frontal arachnoid endothelioma (meningioma). *Neuropsychologia*, 1964, *4*, pp. 257–280.

D-49.   Pribram, K. H., Ahumada, A., Hartog, J., & Roos, L. A progress report on the neurological process disturbed by frontal lesions in primates. In S. M. Warren & K. Akart (Eds.), *The frontal granular cortex and behavior.* New York: McGraw-Hill, 1964. pp. 28–55.

D-53.   Poppen, R., Pribram, K. H. & Robinson, R. S. The effects of frontal lobotomy in man on performance of a multiple choice task. *Exp. Neurol.*, 1965, *11*, pp. 187–229.

D-59.   Pribram, K. H., Konrad, K. & Gainsburg, D. Frontal lesions and behavioral instability. *J. Comp. Physiol. Psychol.*, 1966, *62*, pp. 123–214.

D-64.   Pribram, K. H. & Tubbs, W. Short-term memory, parsing and primate frontal cortex. *Science*, 1967, *156*, p. 1765.

D-67.   Grueninger, W. & Pribram, K. H. The effects of spatial and nonspatial distractors on performance latency of monkeys with frontal lesions. *J. Comp. Physiol. Psychol.*, 1969, *68*, pp. 203–204.

D-77.   Konow, A. & Pribram, K. H. Error recognition and utilization produced by injury to the frontal cortex in man. *Neuropsychologia*, 1970, *8*, pp. 489–491.

D-94.   Anderson, R. M., Hunt, S. C., Vander Stoep, A. & Pribram, K. H. Object permanency and delayed response as spatial context in monkeys with frontal lesions. *Neuropsychologia*, 1976, *14*, pp. 481–490.

D-95.   Pribram, K.H., Plotkin, H. C., Anderson, R. M. & Leong, D. Information sources in the delayed alternation task for normal and "frontal" monkeys. *Neuropsychologia*, 1977, *15*, pp. 329–340.

D-100. Brody, B. A. & Pribram, K. H. The role of frontal and parietal cortex in cognitive processing: Tests of spatial and sequence functions. *Brain*, 1978, *101*, pp. 607–633.

D-110. Prigatano, G. P. & Pribram, K. H. Perception and memory of facial affect following brain injury. *Percep. & Motor Skills*, 1982, *54*, pp. 859–869.

NLP-2. Pinto-Hamuy, T. & Linck, P. Effect of frontal lesions on performance of sequential tasks by monkeys. *Exp. Neurol.*, 1965, *54*, pp. 96–107.

NLP-38. Tubbs, W. E. Primate frontal lesions and the temporal structure of behavior. *Behav. Sci.*, 1969, *14*, pp. 179–184.

C. Posterior

D-23.   Pribram, K. H. & Mishkin, M. Simultaneous and successive visual discrimination by monkeys with inferotemporal lesions. *J. Comp. Physiol. Psychol.*, 1955, *48*, pp. 198–202.

D-38.   Wilson, M., Stamm, J. S., & Pribram, K. H. Deficits in roughness discrimination after posterior parietal lesions in monkeys. *J. Comp. Physiol. Psychol.*, 1960, *53*, pp. 535–539.

D-97.   Ungerleider, L., Ganz, L. & Pribram, K. H. Deficits in size constancy discrimination: Further evidence for dissociation between monkeys with inferotemporal and prestriate lesions. *Exp. Brain Res.*, 1977, *27*, pp. 257–269.

D-99.   Ungerleider, L. & Pribram, K. H. Inferotemporal versus combined pulvinar-prestriate lesions in the rhesus monkey: Effects on color, object and pattern discrimination. *Neuropsychologia*, 1977, *15*, pp. 481–498.

D-101.   Christensen, C. A. & Pribram, K. H. The effect of inferotemporal or foveal prestriate ablation on serial reversal learning in monkeys. *Neuropsychologia*, 1979, *17*, pp. 1–10.

D-104.   Pribram, K. H., Spevack, A., Blower, D. & McGuinness, D. A decisional analysis of the effects of inferotemporal lesions in the rhesus monkey. *J. Comp. Physiol. Psychol.*, 1980, *94*, pp. 675–690.

D-108.   Ruff, R. M., Hersh, N. A. & Pribram, K. H. Auditory spatial deficits in the personal and extrapersonal frames of reference due to cortical lesions. *Neuropsychologia*, 1981, *19*, pp. 435–443.

NLP-3.   Blehert, S. R. Pattern discrimination learning with rhesus monkeys. *Psychol. Reports*, 1966, *19*, pp. 311–324.

NLP-9.   Dewson, J. H., III, Werthein, G. A. & Lynch, J. C. Progressive acquisition of visual pattern discrimination by monkeys. *Percept. Motor Skills*, 1967, *24*, pp. 451–454.

NLP-18.   Dewson, J. H., III, Werthein, G. A. & Lynch, J. C. Acquisition of successive auditory discrimination in monkeys. *J. Acoust. Soc. Amer.*, 1968, *43*, pp. 162–163.

NLP-21.   Wegener, J. G. The effect of cortical lesions on auditory and visual discrimination behavior in monkeys. *Cortex*, 1968, *IV*, pp. 203–232.

NLP-27.   Dewson, J. H., III, & Cowey, A. Discrimination of auditory sequences by monkeys. *Nature*, 1969, *222*, pp. 695–697.

NLP-44.   Ungerleider, L. G. & Brody, B. A. Extrapersonal spatial orientation: The role of posterior parietal, anterior frontal, and inferotemporal cortex. *Exp. Neurol.*, 1977, *56*, pp. 265–280.

D. Sensory-motor

D-26.   Pribram, K. H., Kruger, L., Robinson, F., & Berman, A. J. The effects of precentral lesions on the behavior of monkeys. *Yale J. Biol. & Med.*, 1955–56, *28*, pp. 428–443.

E. Technique

D-42.   Pribram, K. H., Gardner, K. W., Pressman, G. L., & Bagshaw, M. H. An automated discrimination apparatus for discrete trial analysis (DADTA). *Psychol. Reports*, 1962, *11*, pp. 247–250.

D-43.   Sherer, G. & Pribram, K. H. Serial frozen section of whole brain. *Psych. Reports*, 1962, *11*, pp. 209–210.

D-73.   Pribram, K. H. DADTA III: Computer control of the experimental analysis of behavior. *Percept. & Motor Skills*, 1969, *29*, pp. 599–608.

D-92.   Drake, K. U. and Pribram, K. H. DADTA IV: A computer based video display and recording system for behavioral testing. In P. B. Brown (Ed.), *Computer terminology in Neuroscience*. New York: Wiley, 1976. pp. 509–528.

D-93.   Ptito, M., Heaton, G. H., Lassonde, M. C. and Pribram, K. H. A recording procedure for chronic microelectrodes in the cat. *Can. Rev. Psychol.*, 1976, *35*, pp. 43–47.

D-109.   Cutcomb, S., Bolster, R. B. & Pribram, K. H. DADTA VI: A minicomputer-based video control system for the analysis of behavioral and electrophysiological data. *Behavior Res. Meth. & Instr.*, 1981, *13*, pp. 337–340.

III. Psychophysiological Effects Related to Brain Systems

A. GSR, heart rate, respiratory rate

D-51.   Kimble, D. P., Bagshaw, M. H. & Pribram, K. H. The GSR of monkeys during orienting and habituation after selective partial ablations of cingulate and frontal cortex. *Neuropsychologia*, 1965, *3*, pp. 121–128.

D-52.   Bagshaw, M. H., Kimble, D. P. & Pribram, K. H. The GSR of monkeys during orienting and habituation and after ablation of the amygdala, hippocampus and inferotemporal cortex. *Neuropsychologia*, 1965, *11*, pp. 111–119.

D-58.   Koepke, J. E. & Pribram, K. H. Habituation of the GSR as a function of stimulus duration and "spontaneous activity." *J. Comp. Physiol. Psychol.*, 1966, *61*, pp. 442–448.

D-65.   Koepke, J. & Pribram, K. H. Habituation of the vasoconstriction response as a function of stimulus duration and anxiety. *J. Comp. Physiol. Psychol.*, 1967, *64*, pp. 502–504.

NLP-12.   Bagshaw, M. H. & Benzies, S. Multiple measures of the orienting reaction and their dissociation after amygdalectomy in monkeys. *Exp. Neurol.*, 1968, *20*, pp. 175–187.

NLP-13.   Bagshaw, M. H. & Coppock, H. W. Galvanic skin response conditioning deficit in amygdalectomized monkeys. *Exp. Neurol.*, 1968, *20*, pp. 188–196.

NLP-14.   Bagshaw, M. H. & Pribram, J. D. Effect of amygdalectomy on stimulus threshold of the monkey. *Exp. Neurol.*, *1968, 20*, pp. 197–202.

NLP-31.   Konrad, K. W. & Bagshaw, M. H. Effects of novel stimuli on cats reared in a restricted environment. *J. Comp. Physiol. Psychol.*, 1970, *70*, pp. 157–164.

B. Eye movements

D-78.   Bagshaw, M. H., Mackworth, N. H. & Pribram, K. H. Method for recording and analyzing visual fixations in the unrestrained monkey. *Percept. & Motor Skills*, 1970, *31*, pp. 219–222.

D-80.   Bagshaw, M. H., Macworth, N. H. & Pribram, K. H. The effect of inferotemporal cortex ablations on eye movements of monkeys during discrimination training. *Int. J. Neurosci.*, 1970, *1*, pp. 153–158.

D-84.   Bagshaw, M. H., Mackworth, N. H. & Pribram, K. H. The effect of resections of the inferotemporal cortex of the amygdala on visual orienting and habituation. *Neuropsychologia*, 1972, *10*, pp. 153–162.

NLP-32.   Mackworth, N. H. & Bagshaw, M. H. Eye catching in adults, children and monkeys: Some experiments in orienting and observing responses. *Perception and Its Disorders*, 1970, *48*, pp. 201–213.

NLP-33.   Mackworth, N. H. & Otto, D. A. Habituation of the visual orienting response in young children. *Percept. Psycho-phys.*, 1970, *7*, pp. 173–178.

NLP-45.   Ungerleider, L. C. & Christensen, C. A. Pulvinar lesions in monkeys produce abnormal scanning of a complex visual array. *Neuropsychologia*, 1979, *17*, pp. 493–501.

C. Endocrines

NLP-1.   Grueninger, W. E., Kimble, D. P., Grueninger, J., & Levine, S. GSR and corticosteroid response in monkeys with frontal ablations. *Neuropsychologia*, 1965, *3*, pp. 205–216.

IV. Electrophysiological Analysis of Brain Systems

A. Evoked potential

D-54.   Spinelli, D. N., Pribram, K. H. & Weingarten, M. Centrifugal optic nerve response evoked by auditory and somatic stimulation. *Exp. Neurol.*, 1965, *12*, pp. 303–319.

D-55.   Spinelli, D. N. & Pribram, K. H. Changes in visual recovery functions produced by temporal lobe stimulations in monkeys. *Electroenceph. Clin. Neurophysiol.*, 1966, *20*, pp. 44–49.

D-60.   Dewson, J. H., III, Nobel, K. W. & Pribram, K. H. Corticofugal influence at cochlear nucleus of the cat: Some effects of ablation of insular-temporal cortex. *Brain Res.*, 1966, *2*, pp. 151–159.

D-62.   Spinelli, D. N. & Pribram, K. H. Changes in visual recovery functions and unit activity produced by frontal and temporal cortex

REVIEW AND THEORY CHAPTERS

T-1.   Pribram, K. H. Psychosurgery in midcentury. *Surgery, Gynecology & Obstetrics*, 1950, *91*, pp. 364–367.

T-2.   Pribram, K. H. Toward a science of neuropsychology (method and data). In R. A. Patton (Ed.), *current trends in psychology and the behavioral sciences*. Pittsburgh: Univ. of Pittsburgh Press, 1954. pp. 115–142.

T-3.   Pribram, K. H. and Kruger, L. Functions of the "olfactory" brain. *Ann. N. Y. Acad. Sci.*, 1954, *54*, pp. 109–138.

T-4.   Pribram, K. H. Neocortical function in behavior. In H. F. Harlow & C. N. Woolsey (Eds.), *Biological and biochemical bases of behavior*. Madison: Univ. Wisconsin Press, 1953. pp. 151–172.

T-5.   Pribram, K. H. Comparative neurology and the evolution of behavior. In A Roe & G. G. Simpson (Eds.), *Behavior and evolution*. New Haven: Yale Univ. Press, 1958. pp. 140–164.

T-6.   Pribram, K. H. The intrinsic systems of the forebrain. In J. Field, H. W. Magoun, & V. E. Hall (Eds.), *Handbook of physiology, neurophysiology II*. Washington, D.C.: American Physiological Soc., 1960. pp. 1323–1324.

T-7.   Pribram, K. H. A review of theory in physiological psychology. *Ann. Rev. Psychol., 1960, 11*, pp. 1–40.

T-12.   Pribram, K. H. Interrelations of psychology and the neurological disciplines. In S. Koch (Ed.), *Psychology: A study of a science*. New York: McGraw-Hill, 1962. pp. 119–157.

T-13.   Pribram, K. H. The neuropsychology of Sigmund Freund. In A. J. Backrach (Ed.), *Experimental foundation of clinical psychology*. New York: Basic Books, 1962. pp. 442–468.

T-14.   Pribram, K. H. Reinforcement revisited: A structural view. In M. Jones (Ed.), *Nebraska Symposium on Motivation*. Lincoln: Univ. of Nebraska Press, 1963. pp. 113–159.

T-17.   Pribram, K. H. Neuropsychology in America. In E. Berelson (Ed.), *The behavioral sciences today*. New York: Basic Books, 1963. pp. 101–111.

T-20.   Pribram, K. H. Proposal for a structural pragmatism: Some neuropsychological considerations of problems in philosophy. In B. Wolman & E. Nagle (Eds.), *Scientific psychology: Principles and approaches*. New York: Basic Books, 1965. pp. 426–459.

T-22.   Pribram, K. H. Some dimensions of remembering: Steps toward a neuropsychological model of memory. In J. Gaito (Ed.), *Macromolecules and behavior*. New York: Academic Press, 1966. pp. 165–187.

T-23.   Pribram, K. H. A neuropsychological analysis of cerebral function: An informal progress report of an experimental program. *Canadian Psychologist,* 1966, *72,* 324–367.

T-27.   Pribram, K. H. The new neurology and the biology of emotion. *American Psychologist,* 1967, *10,* pp. 830–838.

T-33.   Pribram, K. H., & Melges, F. T. Psychophysiological basis of emotion. In P. J. Vinkey & G. S. Gruyn (Eds.), *Handbook of clinical neurology.* Vol. 3. Amsterdam: North-Holland, 1969. pp. 316–342.

T-34.   Pribram, K. H. The neurophysiology of remembering. *Scientific American,* 1969, pp. 73–86.

T-35.   Pribram, K. H. The neurobehavioral analysis of limbic forebrain mechanisms: Revision and progress report. In D. S. Lehrman, R. A. Hinde, & E. Shaw (Eds.), *Advances in the study of behavior.* New York: Academic Press, 1969. pp. 297–332.

T-36.   Pribram, K. H. Neural servosystems and the structure of personality. *J. Nerv. Ment. Dis.,* 1969, *149,* pp. 30–39.

T-37.   Pribram, K. H. The primate frontal cortex. *Neuropsychologia,* 1969, *7,* pp. 259–266.

T-38.   Pribram, K. H. Four R's of remembering. In K. H. Pribram (Ed.), *The biology of learning.* New York: Harcourt, Brace & World, 1969. pp. 191–225.

T-39.   Pribram, K. H. The amnestic syndromes: Disturbance in coding? In G. A. Talland & M. Waugh (Eds.), *The psychopathology of memory.* New York: Academic Press, 1969. pp. 127–157.

T-42.   Pribram, K. H. Feelings as monitors. In M. B. Arnold (Ed.), *Feelings and emotions.* New York: Academic Press, 1970. pp. 41–53.

T-44.   Pribram, K. H. The biology of mind: Neurobehavioral foundations. In R. A. Gilgen (Ed.), *Scientific psychology: some perspectives.* New York: Academic Press, 1970. pp. 45–70.

T-48.   Pribram, K. H. The realization of mind. *Synthese,* 1971, *22,* pp. 313–322.

T-49.   Pribram, K. H. Autism: A deficiency in context-dependent processes? *Proc. Conf. & Ann. Mtg. of Soc. for Autistic Children,* Public Health Service Bull. #3164, 1971. pp. 42–50.

T-51.   Pribram, K. H. The brain. *Psychology Today,* 1971, *5,* pp. 44–90.

T-53.   Pribram, K. H. Neurological notes on knowing. In J. Royce (Ed.), *The Second Banff Conf. on Theoretical Psych.* New York: Gordon & Breach, 1972. pp. 449–480.

T-56.   Pribram, K. H. Association: Cortico-cortical and/or cortico-subcortical. In T. Frigyesi, E. Rinvik, & M. D. Yahr (Eds.),

tion of knowledge: Making knowledge serve human betterment. Boulder, Co.: Westview Press, 1983. pp. 29–40.

T-144.   Pribram, K. H. Mind and brain, psychology and neuroscience, the eternal verities. In S. Koch & D. E. Leary (Eds.), *A century of psychology as a science.* New York: McGraw-Hill, in press.

T-146.   Pribram, K. H. & McGuinness, D. Brain systems involved in attention related processing. In D. Sheer (Ed.), *Houston Symp. on Attention.* New York: Academic Press, in press.

T-149.   Pribram, K. H. & Robinson, D. Biological contributions to the development of psychology. In C. Buxton (Ed.), *A history of modern psychology; Concepts, methods, viewpoint.* New York: Academic Press, in press.

T-153.   Pribram, K. H. Emotions: A neurobehavioral analysis. In P. Ekman (Ed.), *Approaches to emotion,* in press.

T-154.   Pribram, K. H. Science and the mind/brain issue. In M. L. Maxwell & C. W. Savage (Eds.), *Science and human knowledge: Essays on Grover Maxwell's world-view,* in press.

T-155.   McGuinness, D., Pribram, K. H. & Pirnazar, M. Upstaging the stage model. In C. N. Alexander & E. Langer (Eds.), *Beyond formal operations: Alternative endpoints to human development.* Oxford Univ. Press, in press.

BOOKS AND MONOGRAPHS

B-1.   Miller, G. A., Galanter, E. & Pribram, K. H. *Plans and Structure of Behavior.* New York: Henry Holt, 1960. (Russian trans., 1964; also in Japanese, German, Spanish, Italian.)

B-2.   Pribram, K. H. (Ed.),
    Brain and Behavior I: Mood, States and Mind.
    Brain and Behavior II: Perception and Action.
    Brain and Behavior III: Memory Mechanisms.
    Brain and Behavior IV: Adaptation.
    London: Penguin, Ltd., 1969.

B-3.   Pribram, K. H. & Broadbent, D. (Eds.), *Biology of Memory.* New York: Academic Press, 1970.

B-4.   Hamburg, D. A., Pribram, K. H. & Stunkard, A. J. (Eds.), *Perception and Its Disorders.* Baltimore: Williams & Wilkins, 1970.

B-5.   Pribram, K. H. *What Makes Man Human.* (39th James Arthur Lecture on the Evolution of the Human Brain, 1970.) New York: American Museum of Natural History, 1971.

B-6.   Pribram, K. H. (Ed.), *Central Processing of Sensory Input. The Neurosciences: Third Study Program.* Cambridge, Mass.: MIT Press, 1974.

B-7.   Pribram, K. H. *Languages of the Brain: Experimental Paradoxes and Principles in Neuropsychology.* Englewood Cliffs, N.J.: Prentice-Hall, 1971; Monterey, Ca.: Brooks/Cole, 1977; New York: Brandon House, 1982.

B-8.   Isaacson, R. L. & Pribram, K. H. (Eds.), *The Hippocampus, Volumes I and II.* New York: Plenum, 1975.

B-9.   Pribram, K. H. & Gill, M. M. *Freud's 'Project' Re-Assessed: Preface to Contemporary Cognitive Theory and Neuropsychology.* New York: Basic Books, 1976.

B-10. Pribram, K. H. *Psychoanalysis and the Natural Sciences: The Brain-Behavior Connection from Freud to the Present.* (Inaugural lecture, Freud Memorial Lectures, May, 1981.) London: University College Press, 1982.

B-11. Pribram, K. H. *Perspectives in Neuropsychology,* in preparation for Elsevier.

  Vol. I: Forebrain Systems Analysis.

  Vol. II: Frontolimbic Forebrain and the Flexible Ordering of Behavior.

  Vol. III: The Posterior Cortical Convexity, Image and Information Processing.

B-12. Pribram, K. H. *Mind in the World of Objects.* New York: Basic Books, in preparation.

B-13. Pribram, K. H. *The Mind Machine.* London: Multimedia Publications, in preparation.

B-14. McGuinness, D., & Pribram, K. H. *Origins of Human Culture: An Evolutionary Perspective.* New York: Paragon House, in preparation.

affair with the rat has broadened our understanding of all animals including man.

   We are indeed fortunate to be able to read and appreciate this brief autobiography.

George H. Collier

Curt Richter

occasional visits from my very busy father. At that time, the last years of the century, there were of course, no TV programs, no movies, no radio, and no general entertainment. From my earliest years I spent much of my time working with all kinds of tools. I also spent some time in my father's factory just watching men do their jobs, and soon learned to do some of the things that the workers did, for instance, start and stop the large motors, which gave me great confidence. At home much time was used in taking clocks and locks apart and putting them together again. I remember using my discarded baby-time tin bath tub to make a furnace. I turned the bathtub upside down and cut a door at one end, and at the top I cut a round hole to hold a piece of ordinary stove pipe. I found that I could start a good fire with paper and wood, and it made me think that I had a real furnace going. I spent much time playing with a small magnet in trying to find out what it could do, and in determining how many nails it would lift. In my first experiment, I attempted to determine whether increasing the load on the armature of the magnet by adding a nail every day (on the armature) would increase the strength of the magnet. A poor idea! But it was an experiment. At an early age I had a pocket knife or occasionally two knives that I used for carving initials on fences and trees. I learned to keep them very sharp on a whetstone.

The great simplicity of my life in the play period makes it possible for me to remember in great detail what I did and thought.

This play period came to an end shortly after my father's death, near the end of my ninth year.

After that, activities in school and home took most of my free time. Also, I began playing with boys in the neighborhood and learned to play baseball and football.

Grade School and High School

In grade school and High School I took an active part in school and social activities; I was very active in sports. In my senior year in High School I was president of the class of about 400 students.

I was always a very poor student, just managing to advance from one grade to the other each year.

Dresden, Germany

Almost at once after my graduation from High School, I set out to go to Dresden, Germany to study engineering. This was in keeping with my father's wish.

The Dresden "Hochschule" was one of the best engineering schools in Germany. Dresden opened up a new world for me. At that time it was one of the most beautiful and interesting cities, and one of the chief cultural centers, of Europe. As students we were given special priviledges in getting seats to hear the operas in the Royal Opera House. A different opera was presented every night throughout the season. We also had priviledges of getting seats at the Royal Theatre, where a different play was put on every night throughout the season. I joined a small sports club that was made up largely of Swiss, Finns, Scandinavians, Austrians, Swedes, and about 30% Germans.

HARVARD COLLEGE

In 1915 about six months after the start of the First World War, I decided to give up engineering and to return to America, entering Harvard College as an unclassified student. I began to search for a new career. Not having been exposed to other lines of work other than engineering, I was now at a great loss, not knowing where to start. I picked courses from the Harvard catalog that I thought might help me find what I wanted to do. I did very poorly in all of the courses that I selected, and actually was put on probation at the end of my first year.

A chance conversation with one of the students called my attention to a course in animal behavior given by Professor Robert Yerkes, who I found out was one of the leading workers in the field of behavior. I had not ever thought of doing anything along this line, but the rather exclusive course, given just for one semester for a small group of about eight students, really made me feel that this was something of interest to me. Professor Yerkes seemed very much pleased with my work and spent much time talking to me about what I wanted to do in life, and where I could do it. He recommended that after graduation I should go to work with Professor John B. Watson, at the John Hopkins University. He told me that Watson was one of the leading men in the study of behavior. I had never heard of him nor of the Johns Hopkins University, but I somehow decided that I would go there if I ever had the chance after graduation. It turned out however, at that time I was in real trouble with the Harvard University's authorities. I had done so poorly in all of my courses that I was still on probation and there was a question of whether I would be able to graduate in June. It turned out, however, that the high mark given to me by Professor Yerkes and the fact that I was a First Lieutenant in the R.O.T.C., in which I was quite active, enabled me to graduate.

At the same time I kept thinking about what to do for a topic for my doctoral thesis. Certainly, I had not come with any definite ideas at all. Clearly, I had to work on something that was available, particularly in or near Dr. Watson's lab.

GRASP REFLEX

Watson was then working on the grasp reflex of newborns. This pehnomenon interested me very much. It seemed almost incredible to me that a newborn baby could hang by one hand from a pencil in Watson's hand for as long as 1/2 minute or longer without any support. In my mind I felt that I could really do a job with this phenomenon. This, of course, was one of Watson's main interests so that for the time being it could not be considered as a research project for me. Some years later after Watson had left Hopkins, the opportunity presented itself for me to start some research on the grasp reflex. My ideas worked out fairly well, so within a span of not too many years, I published more than 15 papers on the grasp reflex and its integration into the central nervous system. Furthermore, I still have, even at this time, much material on the grasp reflex that has not been published.

SYMPATHETIC NERVOUS SYSTEM

A further possibility for my doctoral thesis developed quite unexpectedly from a conversation with Professor Meyer. One day Dr. Meyer stopped me in the lobby of the Phipps and told me that some years prior he had purchased a Hindle string galvanometer for Stanley Cobb, who was then his main assistant. Dr. Cobb had not been able to use the instrument at all before he was called to a professorship at Harvard. Dr. Meyer then asked me if it would interest me to do anything with this instrument. I told him that I really did not know too much about it, but that I certainly would like to try to use it. He then had this impressive looking instrument sent to my room in Watson's lab. It was about 12 ft. long with an enormous magnetic coil and camera, and other small parts. I did know that galvanometers of various types had been used for the study of the so-called psychogalvanic reflex. This definitely made it a candidate for my doctoral thesis, and I learned how to operate it in testing the emotional responses of quite a number of patients in the Phipps Clinic. I found that some patients did not show any responses at all; most of them showed very regular responses. When I followed up this observation I found that the patients that did not show any responses at all had a very high level of electrical resistance of the skin, which I could measure very easily and accurately.

Although this was an interesting area to work on, it would involve too much work for a doctoral thesis, and I therefore put the galvanometer out of my mind to work on my doctoral thesis. I did pick it up later and found many interesting differences between patients, and many interesting differences in the electrical resistance of the skin of animals. All together I have published about 75 papers on skin resistance, which I found in the end gave a very accurate and simple measure of activity in the sympathetic nervous system.

NORWAY RAT

This then left rats as subjects for my thesis. Dr. Watson had placed a cage of 12 rats in my room. I did not know whether he had them put there to give me some idea of what to do for my doctoral thesis, or whether he put them there just to keep me company while I was wrestling around with myself to find a good subject. He did not know that I did not have any experience at all with handling rats, either domesticated or wild rats. As a matter of fact, none of my friends in Denver ever had rats as pets, so I never really had an opportunity even to hold a rat. After overcoming a considerable amount of anxiety about handling them, I did succeed in getting the 12 rats out of the one large cage and putting them in 12 smaller cages and then making sure they all had bread and milk that Watson had left for them. What impressed me most of all about the rats was their spontaneous activity: the fact that they just jumped all around over the cage and climbed around for periods and then were quiet again. I could not help but wonder what made them active. So then, I decided to make a study of their activity, first of all to record it in a simple way, and then to correlate it with changes in the animals, whether internal or external. I set about building cages that would record every slight movement of the rats, and would be very sensitive to any kind of activity. This involved quite a bit of experimenting with cages, but it left no doubt in my mind that the "play time period" in the early years of my life helped a great deal in building these cages and

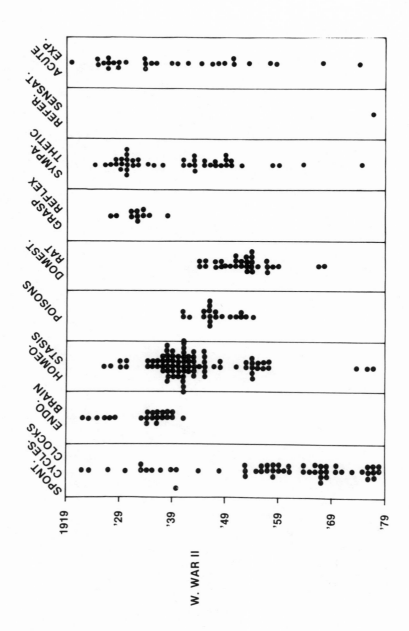

laboratory and arranged to provide all necessary help and funds for the experiments.

PROFESSOR ADOLF MEYER

From the very beginning of my life at the Hopkins, Professor Meyer helped me in every way possible. He supported everything that I wanted to do, not only in the laboratory, but in other parts of the Phipps, for any project I had in mind. When I look back at this period I cannot help but marvel at the wonderful opportunities that he provided for me. During the 20 years or more, I never had to write a grant application for funds or anything. All I had to do was to give the bills to Dr. Meyer's secretary.

This certainly differs markedly from the present time, when most of my friends spend a month or sometimes longer each year simply writing applications for funds.

COLLEAGUES IN OTHER DEPARTMENTS OF THE HOSPITAL

Collaboration with members of the different departments of the Hospital, such as surgery, medicine, pediatrics, anatomy, and physiology, soon became very active. Before long I was publishing papers with members of almost every department.

My experiments began branching out from the rat to almost every other animal and to many types of patients.

The chart in Figure 1 shows the number of papers published over a period from 1922 to 1978. It also shows the distribution of interest in the lab. Certainly, one effect of the release of my gene by Watson was that I began setting up hypotheses on everything that I saw, and further worked out methods of trying to check these hypotheses.

One of the most satisfying results of our various studies was the finding of the great ability of the rat to make dietary selections that result in survival.

GENERAL SUMMARY

1. I had no training either as an undergraduate or a graduate student, in areas that later became my life work such as anat-

17. Richter, C. P. Heavy water as a tool for study of the forces that control length of period of the 24-hour clock of the hamster. Proc. Nat. Acad. Sci. *74*:1295–1299, 1977.

18. Richter, C. P. Discovery of fire by man- its effects on his 24-hour clock and intellectual and cultural evolution. Johns Hopk. Med. J. *141*:47–61, 1977.

19. Richter, C. P. Evidence for existence of a yearly clock in surgically and self-blinded chipmunks. Proc. Nat. Acad. Sci. *75*:3517–3521, 1978.

20. Richter, C. P. Growth hormone 3.6-h pulsatile secretion and feeding times have similar periods in rats. Am. J. Physiol. *239*:(Endocrinol. Metab. 2):E1-E2, 1980.

21. Richter, C. P. Optic Nerve Sectioning in Rats. Brain Res. Bull. *1*:493–494, 1976.

Homeostasis

1. Richter, C. P. A study of the effect of moderate doses of alcohol on the growth and behavior of the rat. J. Exper. Zool. *44*:397–418, 1926.

2. Richter, C. P. and Campbell, K. H. Alcohol taste thresholds and concentrations of solutions preferred by rats. Sci. *91*:507–508, 1940.

3. Richter, C. P. Alcohol as a food. Quart. J. Studies on Alcohol. *1*:650–662, 1941.

4. Richter, C. P. Increased salt appetite in adrenalectomized rats. Am. J. Physiol. *115*:155–161, 1936.

5. Wilkens, and Richter, C. P. A great craving for salt by a child with cortico-adrenal insufficiency. J.A.M.A. *114*:866–868, 1940.

6. Richter, C. P. Salt appetite of mammals: its dependence on instinct and metabolism. Contribution to Vol. 1 "instinct dans le comportement des animaux et de l 'homme' Paris, France, 1956.

Parathyroidectomy—Mineral, Calcium & Phosphorus Appetite

1. Richter, C. P., and Eckert, J. F. Increased calcium appetite of parathyroidectomized rats. Endocrinol. *21*:50–54, 1937.

2. Richter, C. P., and Eckert, J. F. Mineral appetite of parathyroidectomized rats. Am. J. Med. Sci. *198*:9–16, 1939. Increased appetite for calcium solution (lactate, acetate, glucinate and nitrate: also for strontium and magnesium solutions).

3. Richter, C. P., and Honeyman, W., and Hunter, H. Behavior and mood cycles apparently related to parathyroid deficiency. J. Neurol. Psychiat. *3*:19–25, 1940.

Single-Food Choice Diets; Single Purified and Whole Foods

1. Richter, C. P. and Barelare, B., Jr. Further observations on the carbohydrate, fat, and protein appetite of vitamin B deficient rats. Am. J. Physiol. *127*:199–210, 1939.

2. Richter, C. P. and Campbell, K. H. Taste thresholds and taste preferences of rats for five common sugars. J. Nutrit. *20*:31–46, 1940.
3. Richter, C. P. The nutritional value of some common carbohydrates, fats, and proteins studied by the single food choice method. Am. J. Physiol. *133*:29–42, 1941.
4. Richter, C. P. and Hawkes, C. D. The dependence of the carbohydrate, fat, and protein appetite of rats on the various components of the vitamin B complex. Am. J. Physiol. *131*:639–649, 1941.
5. Richter, C. P. Total self-regulatory functions in animals and human beings. Harvey Lecture Series. *38*:63–103, 1942.
6. Richter, C. P. and Rice, K. K. Effects produced by vitamin D on energy, appetite, and oestrous cycles of rats kept on an exclusive diet of yellow corn. Am. J.Physiol. *139*:693, 1943.
7. Richter, C. P. Six common sugars as tools for the study of appetite for sugar. *Taste and Development: The Genesis of Sweet Preference* edited by James M. Weiffenbach, Ph.D. National Institute of Dental Research, DHEW Publication No. (NIH) 77-1068, U. S. Department of Health, Education and Welfare, National Institute of Health, Maryland, 1977.

Diabetes Insipidus, Thirst and the Pituitary Gland

1. Richter, C. P. and Eckert, J. F. Further evidence for the primacy of polyuria in diabetes insipidus. Am. J. Physiol. *113*:578–581, 1935.
2. Richter, C. P. Factors determining voluntary ingestion of water in normals and in individuals with maximum diabetes insipidus. Am. J. Physiol. *122*:No. 3, June, 1938.

Self-Selection Studies

1. Richter, C. P., and Eckert, J. F. Mineral metabolism of adrenalectomized rats studied by the appetite method. Endocrinol. *22*:214–224, 1938.
2. Richter, C. P. Animal behavior and internal drives. Quart. Rev. Biol. *2*: 307–343, 1927.
3. Richter, C. P., and Holt, L. E., Jr., Barelare, B., Jr., and Hawkes, C. D. Changes in fat, carbohydrate, and protein appetite in vitamin B deficiency. Am. J. Physiol. *124*:596–602, 1938.
4. Richter, C. P. and Schmidt, E. C. H., Jr. Behavior and anatomical changes reproduced in rats by pancreatectomy. Endocrinol. *25*:698–706, 1939.
5. Richter, C. P. Behavior and endocrine regulators of the internal environment. Endocrinol. *28*:193–195, 1941.
6. Richter, C. P. and Schmidt, E.C. H., Jr. Increased fat and decreased carbohydrate appetite of pancreatectomized rats. Endocrinol. *28*:179–192, 1941.
7. Richter, C. P. Biology of drives. Psychosomatic Medicine. *3*:105–110, 1941.
8. Richter, C. P. Total self-regulatory functions in animals and human beings. Harvey Lecture Series. *38*:63–103, 1942, 1943.